Bob Hayes

Wolves of the Yukon

This book is dedicated to my parents,

Leonard and Eileen Hayes,

and to my wife, Caroline Hayes

Wolves of the Yukon

Published in 2010

by Bob Hayes

All rights reserved © Bob Hayes 2010

Printed in Germany

Druckerei Fritz Kriechbaumer

Wettersteinstraße 12, 82024 Taufkirchen

ISBN: 978-09867376-0-2

Contents

Foreword

Wolves. The images that this word brings to mind vary tremendously around the world, both in scope and in their nature. This usually relates to what we have read ("Wolves Kill 30 Sheep"), seen in photos (what a marvelous looking animal....), or been told. But for a relatively few, also to what we have encountered where wolves actually occur.

My first encounter was from the back of a small airplane circling over a sleeping pack in forested northeastern Minnesota. That evening, from a cold, snow-packed trail less than a mile from those same wolves, a human howled into a still, black night and elicited a mournful, wild reply. After that, fate and a bit of determination put me on track to spend subsequent summers and then years studying wolves and their prey in several different places. Now, my own image of wolves is tempered by having caught and collared them, watched them from airplanes, collected and analyzed data that helped me understand them, and dealt with people who had intense feelings for them, both good and bad.

And to this extent, I certainly have an affinity to Bob Hayes and his experiences with wolves, the subject of this book. I passed through the Yukon one summer during college while driving to and from Alaska, and I remember endless black spruce forests, rugged mountains with a few white sheep specks, few but friendly people, and gorgeous northern lights. It also turned out that I first saw Dall's sheep up close much later in life when I hiked with Bob and families high on the alpine tundra above Kusawa Lake in the southern Yukon, not far, I think, from his introductory narrative of wolves hunting sheep in Chapter 11. We had camped on the edge of the lake, a long boat ride from the nearest road access with no one else for miles around. It was a magnificent setting in a spectacular place, and the short time spent there and a few other locales in the Yukon made me appreciate even more this special place and the wolf biologist who thrived there.

Bob's captivating historical overview of the Yukon from the wolf's perspective is an auspicious beginning that sparks one's imagination of what used to be. The interactions with the first humans in the Yukon give perspective to those which have followed, and helps one better understand the very recent and current circumstances under which wolf "management" has attempted to control this wild place. But because of low human density and a relatively light human "footprint", the wilderness of the Yukon still provides a full complement of indigenous flora and fauna and natural processes. And because of its diversity, it is a microcosm of wolf/prey interactions throughout much of their northern hemispheric range. As Bob chronicles, wolves prey on migrating caribou on the tundra, hunt moose in thick spruce forests, and chase sheep on sheer mountain cliffs. From a scientist's point of view, the circumstances of studying wolves in such a place are enviable. More importantly, the insights that Bob and colleagues have generated over the years have added importantly to the ability of we humans to intelligently interact with wolves and the systems in which they live. That is one major lesson of this book. Another is that it is a rare and valuable thing to have the opportunity to spend such time learning about wildlife, whether wolves or wagtails, and to make the most out of such chances. Bob Hayes certainly accomplished that, as well.

One lingering, pebble-in-my-shoe thought that has arisen as a result of reading this book has to do with wild places, in general, and how we experience them (or don't, for many of the current generation). Many wolf biologists of Bob's and my generation also took advantage of what was, at the beginning of our careers, a high-tech innovation called radio-telemetry. The benefit it provided was that we could jump in an airplane or helicopter and find marked wolves almost anytime we wanted to, watch them for a minute or two, and then move on to the next pack. It afforded the opportunity to collect significantly more data of certain kinds, and to generate tables and graphs that helped answer many questions more confidently. We caught wolves, handled them, followed tracks, investigated kill sites and den sites, and picked up scats. But I think previous generations of wolf biologists likely scoffed a bit, and even shook their heads in sorrow, at what we, the new guys, were losing by not spending even more time on the ground, like they did, collecting information the old-fashioned way, and experiencing the world of the wolf in a much more intimate way, albeit more slowly and deliberately. The "pebble" is that students I help today now often mark large mammals with satellite-connected collars and monitor nearly real-time hourly movements at their desk, then make inferences about locations of kill sites and test new ideas about travel paths and habitat use. But I think they are losing even more of the connection with the real environment than I did, and so I scoff and shake my head in sorrow. "Go to the Yukon," I should tell them, "and experience what the natural world is really like... and if not, then read this book and you'll yearn to go."

Todd Fuller, Professor of Wildlife Conservation, University of Massachusetts - Amherst

Preface

The wolf is the most studied large mammal on earth and there are more books written about them than just about any other animal. So why write another one? As a biologist for the Yukon government, I had the fortune of studying wolves for almost twenty years and learned a lot about them. I have come to understand that the Yukon wolf story is unique and needs to be told. By sharing what I have learned about this exceptional carnivore I will hopefully help others understand more about the wolf's role in the natural and human history of the Yukon.

Wolves are the primary natural force that has shaped and animated the Yukon wilderness through the last ice age to today. They are the key predator controlling and keeping Yukon moose and caribou populations in check. The Yukon wolf is also an important mythological animal to native peoples, and a central foundation of the culture, social system, spiritual world, and story myths of many tribes. But there is more. The evolution of the wolf as the symbol of wilderness – and our very perception of what is wild – first came from the imagination of a young writer who spent a brief winter in the Yukon at the turn of the twentieth century.

In addition, much of the history of the Yukon since the gold rush was shaped by our insatiable competition with wolves for wild game. Wolves rival the importance of the Klondike gold fields in driving the politics and economy of the Yukon Territory during the twentieth century. In nearly all decades the Yukon government found ways to kill wolves, mainly to benefit trappers and big game outfitters. Controlling wolves either by bounty, poison, trapping, aerial shooting – and eventually even fertility control – was a main activity of a steady list of Yukon territorial governments since 1901. In short, the wolf is the fuel that fires the Yukon wilderness.

I am a wildlife biologist. I learned about the wild behavior of wolves by studying hundreds of them in the field for two decades. I have written a stack of scientific reports in my career, but most people find them a bit boring. Science research includes hypotheses, methods, discussion, and conclusions all based on logical argument that is written in a way to help convince other biologists they are reading the 'truth' – at least as far as science is concerned. Unfortunately, good science has little to do with good writing. So, no matter how I arranged or stacked my publications they could never really tell what I have learned, what I know, what I think, and especially how I feel about wolves. To tell my story I wrote this book. I had to shift away from presenting precise facts and arguments, and allow myself to write about what I know and think and feel. This shift was hard at first with many drafts and deleted files to show for it. I hope this book captures what I intended to say.

There is a Chinese proverb that goes, "*Tell me and I'll forget; show me and I may remember; involve me and I'll understand.*" I introduce each chapter with a narrative or short story. Here I have freely mixed real wolf events I have seen with historical fiction to spark and engage your imagination and interest. My hope is that by the end of the book you will understand more about the biology of the wolf and how this exceptional predator – and ultimately we humans – fit into the Yukon landscape, the very last remaining mountain wilderness of North America.

For the prehistoric chapters I have had to imagine the wolf and where it fits into this ancient world through narratives. Most stories are based on real wolf behavior I have seen in the wild. Some events are based on what other biologists have written down or told me about. My imaginary events, or ones like them, probably happened long ago because the modern Yukon wolf – *Canis lupus* – is similar to the ancient wolf of the past. How modern wolves behave today can help us reconstruct an understanding of how wolves lived in the Yukon long before there were people in the landscape.

The first section of the book is about history. We will take a journey through Yukon time and space, and the wolf is our vehicle. The journey begins at the height of the last ice age. Wolves roamed the vast ice-free plains of Beringia preying on a multitude of large mammals and competing for the spoils with some of the most dangerous large predators that ever lived. The second chapter is set on the Old Crow Flats 12,500 years ago; a time when the landscape and plant communities were rapidly changing and the wolf faced the greatest extinction of mammals ever known. Chapter Three is set 7,500 years ago – after the great continental ice sheets had disappeared and forests were spreading through the Yukon. The land was filled with caribou and a host of new mammals including elk, bison and moose. The fourth chapter explores the idea of the wolf as 'provider' to Yukon native peoples, and why it became important in mythology and a spiritual animal for many tribes. In Chapter Five, I have invented a fictional encounter on the frozen Yukon River during the Klondike gold rush between a pack of wolves and Jack London, a writer who went on to shape our collective notions about wilderness. Chapters Six and Seven follow social change in the Yukon from 1900 to the 1970's when people regularly turned against the wolf using bounties, bullets, and strychnine to reduce competition by wolves for valuable fur and big game.

The second part of the book is titled Understanding. It focuses on the things I have learned from studying Yukon wolves. These chapters explore the relations between wolves and caribou, Dall's sheep, and moose – their main prey. There are also chapters about how wolves interact and compete with ravens and also grizzly bears – their archrivals. We will go inside the cockpits of planes and helicopters to see how my team snow-tracked wolves in winter and captured and radio-collared wolves to study their movements, predatory behavior, and survival. Another chapter explores the relation between wolves and water, an often overlooked, but critical element of Yukon wolf habitat. The last chapter is about contemporary wolf control. I was part of three such programs between 1982 and 2000. As a biologist, I helped find and shoot wolves from the air, but I also pressured the end of a government poison campaign, and I pioneered the first non-lethal methods to control wolf numbers more humanely. I will explain why I no longer believe that broad scale killing of wolves is biologically justified and the wrong thing to do to increase moose and caribou populations for people.

So, to begin, let's return 20,000 years to a desolate, wind-scoured mountain ridge at the edge of the living world. There is an ancient wolf pack on it.

Part 1 History

1

The Mammoth Steppe

Two Ocean Creek · 20,000 years ago

The pack is moving single file along a windswept mountain ridge at the northeastern tip of the Beringia steppe. The leader, a gray female, stops and gently presses her nose to the ground. The scent is no longer on the ridge. She backtracks a few meters and finds it again, then she heads downhill followed by her five young. Two are pups, mostly grown. The other three are her yearlings. Her mate is somewhere below hidden by a swirling cloud of glacial dust that spins hundreds of meters in the air. She picks up her pace trying to stay with the rapidly fading scent. Suddenly a great blast of brown dust forms a wild, twisting cloud high above the ridge.

Five kilometers away is the origin of the wind. A massive wall of ice fills the east horizon. The long, flowing glacier snakes out onto the valley floor below, compressed and squeezed by the titanic weight of the immense ice sheet. At the glacier's sides and front lies an enormous jumble of massive rocks, gravel, and dirt debris mixed in the brilliant, aquamarine ice. The peaks of the highest mountains are all that rise above the endless sea of ice.

The family moves down the ridge and swings out onto a treeless plain. As they head away from the great wall of ice, the ground begins to show signs of life. Here the soil is new and thin – only the smallest and hardiest plant life can anchor in. Meadows of grass and pasture sage are scattered along the dry gravel benches and cover the exposed hillsides. The hardy stems of purple pentstemon flowers, their petals long since gone, blow among the small boulders and gravel pans. Soon the pack catches up with the male who has slowed down to check a fresh scent. Prey has passed here not long ago. The female now takes the lead winding through the rolling steppe filled with small melt-water ponds and lakes. She stops often, checking the wind but the scent has vanished.

The wolves lie down at the base of a small hill to rest. In minutes they are all sleeping; their backs to the strong, cold wind. But the female is hungry and is restless. She slowly moves to the hilltop where she has a view of the open plain ahead. The male soon follows her. Sensing their parents are gone, the young wake and head uphill. Soon the pack is huddled together and sleeping as the red sun drops below the horizon.

By morning they are all hungry. Their last meal was two days ago – a horse foal they killed and devoured in minutes. The male moves down the hill and the others soon follow. He begins to walk briskly along the edge of an ancient dry riverbed. Before long there is the unmistakable smell of caribou. The pack stops to fix where the scent is coming from. It is fresh and close by. The wolves are excited but they remain silent, moving quietly but quickly ahead.

The bull does not hear them coming but it stops grazing when it feels the soft vibration of animals moving on gravel. As the wolves approach, it raises its head showing the large rack of antlers. Its heart is instantly racing as the adrenalin courses to its muscles preparing to run. The wolves instinctively spread out and silently watch the motionless bull. The female attacks first, and her mate follows. The others watch as the two adults slowly circle the caribou testing for any advantage. The bull drops its head slowly and swings its great antlers at the wolves. It is too late to run.

The female darts in behind the caribou and works the back thighs. She is careful to dodge the antlers when the bull swings toward her. The male sees his chance and springs forward gripping onto a shoulder. His canines sink deep in the flesh and he holds on for a few seconds before the bull swings its thick neck back, shaking his grip. The wolves can easily avoid the antlers and begin circling the injured bull once more. Blood wells from a severed vein high on the shoulder.

The caribou shakes its head, confused by this two-sided attack. Desperate, it lowers its head and charges for the male. The wolf deftly spins sideways, avoiding the sharp points. As the bull begins to raise its head the male clamps its teeth into the long soft snout. Instantly the female tears into the flesh of the left flank and holds firm. In a final adrenaline-fueled gesture, the bull lifts both wolves off the ground and spins them in a short arc before collapsing on its side. The young wolves all rush onto the dying bull. The adults feed first. The male tears into the steaming gut and snaps out a lobe of liver, bolting down the bloody prize in a few seconds. He steps back, brushing the shoulder of the female as she rips away the thin diaphragm muscle containing the heart. She snaps and growls at her mate then removes the heart in a few bites. She stands in the gut and licks the heavy pool of blood welling in the cavity. The young wolves pace anxiously a few meters away. The pups get their chance to feast with the parents, but both adults still snap and bare their teeth at them in an age-old ritual of ownership. Eventually the satiated adults wander off carrying meat prizes. The yearlings instantly rush in growling and snapping their canines, pushing the pups aside. The male – blood stained to the waist – climbs a low hill and lies down. He eats his prize slowly sometimes looking out over the open steppe. He rises quickly when he sees a large shape moving through the gravel wash below.

The giant short-faced bear comes downwind. It is huge, weighing more than nine hundred kilograms. It can move surprising fast for its massive size. Standing on hind legs the bear swings its great head slowly back and forth trying to isolate the fresh smell of death in the wind. By now the pack has seen the coming bear and they are all barking frantically. The bear raises it great head sniffing deeply. He finds his bearings, drops, and silently charges. The wolves hold ground briefly but panic in all directions when the huge bear is suddenly upon them. The bear bounds onto the carcass and spins around, roaring and slamming its massive forelegs into the ground daring any challenge for the prize between its legs. But the bear is an impossible opponent – twenty times larger than the wolves.

Undaunted, the male wolf attacks from behind, leaping onto the bear's massive shoulder. The bear roars and spins sharply but cannot shake the wolf off. The female sees her chance and joins in locking onto the bear's back leg. The bear swings hard, driving its powerful foreleg into the male's side. The blow drives the tumbling wolf back into the gravel. Then the bear kicks at the female sending her sprawling in the other direction. The male regains his feet and charges the bear again, snapping at the great legs. The female rushes forward but loses her courage. She retreats back to her frantically barking young. It is over.

The two adults face the bear, their heads low, teeth bared. The excited juveniles bark wildly behind. The bear bluff charges the pack, and they scatter once more. It moves back onto the caribou straddling the carcass again. It roars a great and final declaration of ownership. The two wolves move away in ever-widening circles until they reach a barren hill where the young wolves have already retreated. The adults join a chorus of staccato barks and howls. The midday wind is blowing stronger now, and the low sounds are carried off onto the open steppe. The bear slices meticulously into the caribou with its razor-sharp claws and it begins to feed.

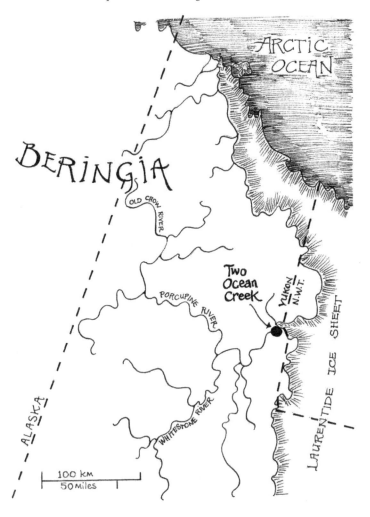

T his 'day in the life' of an ancient wolf pack is from a composite of real wolves and events I have seen. In the 1980s, I studied the Two-Ocean Creek wolf pack in the northeast Yukon. The pack's territory was the Rat River drainage of the Northern Richardson Mountains – the very same mountains that blocked the westward advance of the great Laurentide ice sheet at the Yukon boundary some 20,000 years ago. I radio-collared the wolves on the same ridge I imagined the ancient wolf pack traveling at the beginning of this chapter. The cover photo shows the Two Ocean Creek wolves just moments before being collared. Today the Laurentide ice sheet has long since disappeared and the mountains are now home to moose, caribou and one of the northernmost groups of Dall's sheep populations.

The last time I saw the Two-Ocean Creek pack a grizzly bear had stumbled out of hibernation and drove the wolves off their caribou kill. I also watched another grizzly steal a moose kill from the Rose Lake pack in the south Yukon. The wolves defended their kill the same way I imagine the Pleistocene wolves combated the giant short-faced bear. In the end the grizzly bear – like the short-faced bear – triumphed and stole the Rose Creek wolves' hard-earned kill.

I watched another wolf pack kill a cow moose in the same way the wolves in the story kill the ancient caribou. As I circled in a small aircraft, I saw the Watson River wolves drive a cow moose from the forest into a small meadow and surround it. In minutes the two adults gripped the snout and rump. The desperate moose lifted the two wolves off the ground and spun them as if they were riding a carousel. Twice she shed the wolves but the last time she collapsed, too exhausted to stand. Fossil evidence shows wolf body size and predatory behavior has remained unchanged since the Pleistocene, making my story believable. But the ice age landscape of the Yukon Pleistocene was remarkably different.

Twenty thousand years ago, the last great ice age was at its peak, burying the temperate regions of North America under a great sea of ice as much as three kilometers thick. The Laurentide ice sheet was so massive it is hard to imagine today. The great sheet stretched four thousand kilometers from the Yukon to the Gulf of St. Lawrence covering all of present-day Canada, and grinding south as far as the state of Wisconsin. The smaller Cordilleran sheet covered all but the highest mountain peaks of Washington, Idaho, Montana, British Columbia, and the south Yukon.

As the ice sheets grew, the seasonal temperature differences became smaller and smaller until summers were too cool to melt the previous winter's snow. For thousands of years snow accumulated until the weight compressed it into hard ice. Over time, the continental sheets thickened and spread until they reached their greatest size about 20,000 years ago. As the earth's water became locked in ice, the ocean levels dropped, forming a broad land bridge between Asia and North America. About the same time the Laurentide and Cordilleran ice sheets fused together along the spine of the Rocky Mountains, forming a great ice barrier that blocked the north-south movement of mammals in North America for many thousand years.

But ice was not everywhere. Tucked in the northwest corner of North America and western Siberia was a vast, ice-free land that included the continental shelf of the Bering Sea that was dry and covered in grasslands. Paleontologists call this ice-free land Beringia. The ice sheets effectively cut off Beringia from the rest of North America, stopping the north-south genetic flow of plants and animals for many thousands of years. For much of the Pleistocene, the ecological connection was between Eurasia and Beringia. Land mammals and plants migrated across the land bridge in both directions. Over time, new Beringia species evolved such as the steppe bison, Beringia lion, and Yukon horse. The mammals that flourished were grazers, or animals that mowed grasses and other low-lying plants for food.

Beringia was a vast treeless plain or steppe resembling the high grassland plateaus of Mongolia today. Wet fens, bogs, and sedge meadows covered the poorly drained lowlands. Grasses, sage and dry tundra forbs covered well-drained areas and the lower slopes of mountains. This grassland supported several large herbivore species at the end of the ice age, evidence of the great richness of the steppe environment even at the coldest period of glaciation. Four grazers ruled the land: the woolly mammoth, steppe bison, horse, and caribou. The muskox, western camel, saiga antelope and Dall's sheep were less common. Most of these fabulous herbivores have since become extinct. But 30,000 to 12,000 years ago the Beringia steppe was filled with large mammals. From fossils, we now know that populations ebbed and flowed depending on climatic conditions and genetic vitality.

Research using radiocarbon analysis has shown that mammoths and horses were the two signature herbivores at the end of the ice age. Bison were present but not as abundant. But what about the big predators, when did they flourish and how did they compete for prey through the Pleistocene? Scientists excavated wolf fossils in the Yukon and Alaska dating back 47,000 years, so we know the wolf lived in Beringia and hunted the mammoth steppe far back in the Pleistocene. What did these wolves look like? Which animals did they hunt? How many wolves were there, and how successful were they?

Paul Matheus is a paleontologist who worked in Alaska and the Yukon. He compared ancient and modern skulls from Yukon and Alaska wolves. He found Pleistocene wolves weighed about the same as modern wolves. An adult male tipped the scale at forty-five kilograms and a female at thirty-eight kilograms. Modern wolves tend to prey on the most abundant animals available, but prey size matters. Let's consider the array of available steppe herbivores and see how a hungry pack of Pleistocene wolves might size them up to hunt – or not.

Imagine a Pleistocene pack hunting a group of woolly mammoths on the steppe. As the wolves move in, all the traits that make them great pursuit hunters – their speed, agility, acute eyesight, and linear frames – have no advantage with these great elephants. The bulls are enormous, weighing more than 7,000 kilograms – more than 200 times larger than a wolf. The huge mammals stop grazing and they casually turn to face the approaching wolves. They continue chewing the rough mat of grass. They are unconcerned by the arrival of the wolf pack. The adults are three meters tall at the shoulder with a well-developed trunk, a high rounded forehead, large curving tusks, and a large dorsal hump. Their bodies are covered with long woolly hair that blows from their flanks in the wind. They slowly swing their long white tusks and trumpet great blasts of air from their trunks – a noisy warning the wolves do not take lightly. After a few minutes a lone cow walks forward slowly to challenge the pack. The alpha male scrambles away to avoid being trampled under her huge legs.

The wolves' teeth are too small to pierce the thick elephant skin, even if they could somehow get through the thick and long hair. One false move, one missed dodge of the huge feet and the wolf will be trampled like a crepe. Instinctively, it registers that for it to pass on its genes to another generation, it will have to abandon these big beasts and find something smaller and easier to kill. The male slowly moves off, knowing it will only be able to scavenge the odd mammoth meal courtesy of a bigger predator, or have the good fortune of stumbling onto a mammoth that has somehow died.

Now imagine the same pack finds a herd of steppe bison a few kilometers away. This is the second largest Beringia mammal weighing in at 800 kilograms. It's smaller than a mammoth but still twenty times the size of these ancient wolves. This challenging meal has two shoulder humps and huge, curved horns – three to four times broader than the horns of modern plains bison. And it is another big mammal that does not run when tested. As the wolves move in the herd forms a great wall of bristling horns, dark faces, snorting nostrils, and stamping feet. Three bulls break from the wall and charge the wolves. The wolves scramble away to safety. This time it will be death by a dozen bison hooves rather than a single mammoth foot. The alpha male decides to avoid these beasts also – at least for now. As the wolves depart he scans the herd for signs of a future chance at a kill – a limp, a wound, a crippled gait, a calf that is faltering behind, or one that is slow to suckle its mother. The wolf finds a cow that is walking slower than the others, a bloody wound weeping from a flank. It will be worthwhile checking back in a few days.

A few miles further the pack crests a low ridge and they hit the jackpot. Below them, hundreds of Yukon horses are milling on the open steppe. The wolves's hunting instincts prickle. This is prey the Beringia wolf was born to hunt. The horses are small, standing about a meter at the shoulders. And they won't stand to defend themselves. They will try to escape by running and they will be very fast. The chances of a meal suddenly improve because next to the horses are hundreds of Beringia caribou lying on a large snow patch, escaping the torment of the summer mosquitoes. These ancient herbivores weigh about one hundred fifty kilograms – about three to four times the wolf's size – and like horses, they are the perfect prey. But caribou are also excellent runners with long legs, streamlined bodies and broad, stable hooves. In a short heat they can outdistance the wolf, but not in the long run. Both horse and caribou are just the right size for a single wolf to pull down. On the run they will expose their flank, shoulders, neck and back to wolf attacks. The wolves are built to run them down with better endurance, great speed, and excellent agility. The pack moves in, careful not to startle the nervous horses, as every step closer is a hunting advantage. The wolves attack suddenly and there is a great chaos of horse and caribou twisting, turning, and scrambling to escape. The ancient hunt begins.

With many smaller herbivores to hunt, the Beringia wolf did not need to go after the big ones. There were caribou and horse, and the other steppe grazers including muskox, saiga antelope, Dall's sheep, and camel. We know from some forensic science that Pleistocene wolves killed horse. Gold miners recently excavated a 26,000 year-old horse carcass near Dawson City. The neck and leg bone has puncture holes that fit exactly the first two impressions of wolf premolars. Besides horse, Pleistocene wolves were certainly capable of killing caribou and even steppe bison. But did the Beringia wolf specialize in hunting a few herbivores, or was it an opportunist hunting whatever it could? To find the answers we need to know what other carnivores were on the steppe. Then we need to find out about what they likely killed.

Near the end of the last ice age, seven Beringia carnivores roamed the mammoth steppe with the wolf. In descending order of size there was the giant short-faced bear, Beringia lion, scimitar cat, grizzly bear, black bear, a small canid called the dhole, and wolverine. The giant short-faced bear tipped the scales at more than 1,000 kilograms – four to five times the size of modern Yukon grizzly bears. The huge bear could kill anything that walked the steppe including adult woolly mammoths. It was also a formidable scavenger easily staking claim to carcasses killed by other carnivores. The bear lived only in North America. Some biologists speculate that humans ventured over the land bridge from Asia only after the short-faced bear disappeared at the end of the last ice age.

The Beringia lion was the next largest carnivore. It was long-limbed and powerful which allowed it to make long chases on the steppe. Adults weighed about 240 kilograms – 25 percent heavier than modern African lions. The Beringia lion lived in large family groups or prides, similar to modern lions. It used its explosive speed and great size to surprise and kill prey as large as steppe bison. The scimitar cat was about the size of a lion but it was more slender weighing 150-250 kilograms. It was also quick and agile, with a long neck and forelegs, and short but powerful hind legs. Its weapon was a pair of large curved canines edged with razor-sharp serrations. The cat ambushed and impaled prey with the large canines, mortally wounding the animals.

Pleistocene grizzly bears were omnivores, meaning they ate plants and animals. Their size and speed made them formidable predators of large mammals. Black bear were present in Beringia during the Pleistocene based on DNA found in some scat in Bear

Cave Mountain in the north Yukon, but it seems they were not common.

Dholes also ranged in Beringia during the late Pleistocene. Weighing 12 – 18 kilograms, this small cousin of the wolf survives today in Asia where it is currently endangered. Like the wolf it is highly social forming large family packs. Modern dholes specialize in killing animals weighing about fifty kilograms. During the Pleistocene the horse would have been ideal prey of the dhole. The wolverine was the last and smallest of the seven Beringia carnivores. It weighed about nine kilograms and, like modern Yukon wolverine, it survived by hunting small birds and mammals, and by scavenging.

To understand what these carnivores ate scientists use a method called isotope analysis. The technique measures the relative amounts of radioactively stable carbon to nitrogen in their bones. The ratio in carnivore bones depends upon the animals they ate. A carnivore that specializes on a single prey species shows an isotope ratio similar to that of its prey. A carnivore that consumes many prey types shows no distinct isotope signature. The radioactive elements have a long life – thousands of years in fact – so isotopes can be used to study diets of ancient predators.

Katherine Fox-Dobbs from the University of California and a team of researchers studied dietary patterns in fossil bones of wolves, short-faced bears, grizzly bears, Beringia lions and scimitar cats during three periods of the late Pleistocene: pre-glacial cold period (50,000 to 23,000 years ago), glacial (23,000 to 18,000 years ago) and the end of the ice age (18,000 to 10,000 years ago). Her team found most predators were general consumers and not specialized hunters on any single herbivore species. Beringia lions, scimitar cats, and grizzly bears ate all types of prey during the glacial period and after the ice age ended, although some scimitar cats specialized on horse or bison. Wolves fed on the widest range of prey matched only by lions after the ice age ended. About half of the wolves specialized on muskox and caribou during the pre-glacial.

Caribou figured in the diet of wolves throughout the Pleistocene showing an ancient predatory relation that continues to this day. While there is evidence of wolf presence in all the Pleistocene periods, other predators came and went. Scimitar cats disappeared about 36,000 years ago; short-faced bear vanished about 20,000 years ago. Beringia lions hung in until about 10,000 years ago then they went extinct. Fox-Dobb's study found that only a few of the five carnivores were ever present on the steppe together at the same time, reducing competition with wolves for prey that also underwent times of high abundance and scarcity.

Isotope studies can tell us what an ancient carnivore ate but they cannot tell if the food was killed or scavenged. To figure out where the predatory wolf fit in the mammoth steppe, we need to look at its physical traits and make some educated guesses about what it was best at hunting.

Wolves are cursorial, which simply means they have a body type that evolved for running quickly. The open steppe is the ideal terrain for open pursuit hunting. The wolf has a light, linear skeletal frame, a large 'rudder' tail for changing direction in a split second, and exceptional stamina to run at top speed for half an hour. It has particularly hard bones that allow the animal to safely twist, turn, and tumble during pursuit with small risk of injury. Most likely the Beringia wolf could outrun many steppe herbivores over open ground.

Pleistocene wolves probably killed animals up to the size of bison. Most grassland herbivores were within the size range of prey that gray wolves kill around the world today. It is easy to imagine Beringia packs killing caribou, horses, muskoxen, mountain sheep, saiga antelope, and camel because they prey on these animals nowadays. The Pleistocene wolf was also well adapted for following these fast moving migrating herds. Being small, it could also move quickly and scavenge from kills made by other larger carnivores on the open grassland. The small size was also an advantage for avoiding being killed by slower, but dangerous Beringia lions, scimitar cats, short-faced bears, and grizzly bears that undoubtedly competed with wolves for carcasses.

Beringia wolves probably formed large packs and were, by nature, migratory year-round. Living in a large pack would have ensured wolves would quickly consume most of the food they killed, leaving little for other carnivores. The mammoth steppe supported many herbivores to prey on, which would also have supported an evolution to large pack sizes. We can look to the modern African hunting dog that forms large packs in the herbivore rich savanna grasslands. These large groups have evolved because there is intense competition from other large carnivores and vultures for any prey the dogs kill. Consuming things quickly is an advantage in any system with high competition for food. Being migratory was an ecological requirement for Beringia wolves because most of the steppe herbivores traveled long distances in search of cyclic grassland forage. In the far north Yukon today, tundra wolves are migratory following the Porcupine caribou herd year-round (See Chapter Twelve).

Considering what we know from the scientific record, we can summarize where the Beringia wolf probably fit into the ecology of the mammoth steppe. Wolf fossils are scattered through Siberia, Alaska, and the Yukon through the entire late Pleistocene, so we can be sure the wolf was both adaptable and successful. The guild of herbivore prey was diverse, with a wide range of prey sizes to exploit. As herbivore populations increased and declined, Beringia wolves found ways to shift predation onto other mammals. The steppe grasslands were the ideal place for the wolf's cursorial hunting lifestyle. With its small and agile body, the Pleistocene wolf was well adapted to following migratory herbivores for long distances. There was a great array of profitable prey to hunt and many other carnivores provided scavenging opportunities for wolves. The end of the Pleistocene was a good time to be a wolf. Then, rather suddenly, the ice age ended. Around 12,000 years ago most of the fabulous steppe mammals disappeared from the Yukon during the greatest extinction of land mammals ever known. What happened to the wolf?

2

The End of Horses

Old Crow Flats - 12,500 years ago

The pack is moving along the great frozen plain hugging the edge of a broad stand of snow-filled willows. The wolves are traveling blindly in a heavy winter storm. It is midday, but the Arctic sun is well below the horizon. The low light casts a soft dull blue hue through the thick veil of falling snow. The alpha male is leading. He pushes through the deep snow with his chest, his snout gliding over the surface always testing for scent of prey. A dozen wolves are strung out behind him carving a heavy trail in the snow. His mate is a few meters behind him. She stops to shake the thick layer of snow that has collected on her back. The other wolves stop and sit down, waiting patiently until she is ready to move again. The land is silent except for a light wind blowing through the high bushes that encircle the open plain. It is snowing so heavily their tracks fill in behind them and disappear in a few minutes.

The male stumbles into the fresh trail before he sees it. Instinctively he presses his nose into the tracks. The scent of horse fills his nostrils. He pushes his snout deeper in the trail sniffing and feeling for sign of direction and freshness. He moves his face carefully to the edges of the track. He feels where the leading edge of the horse's foot has compressed and hardened the snow ever so slightly. The scent is strongest on the same edge. He moves to the next trail and confirms direction. The horses are moving out onto the open plain. The wolf cannot see further than a few meters ahead in the heavy blizzard. The other wolves spread out excitedly through the fresh tracks wagging their tails and burying their snouts into the sweet aroma of horse. The pack swings out onto the snowy plain, their pace much quicker now.

A maze of deep drifts slows the progress of the twenty horses. They are moving into a strong wind and cannot smell the danger silently closing in from behind. The pack is moving quickly in the deep horse trails, and they soon close the gap. The first horse to die is trailing fifty meters behind the others. The first wolf collides into the rear of the startled horse before it appears through the blinding blizzard. The tiny stallion rears up in panic, plunging headlong into a soft drift. The wolf instinctively grabs the horse's neck tearing out the jugular vein with a powerful bite. The wolf shifts its fatal grip around the trachea, pulling the horse down, slowly suffocating the small stallion as it kicks vainly in the soft snow. The other wolves rush past and vanish in the snowy whiteness. Just ahead they hear the clattering of many hooves scrambling over ice.

The horses have sensed the coming danger and are charging blindly over the plain through a series of frozen ponds. A young stallion slips and falls on the ice, unable to regain its feet. It is spinning in a slow arc on the ice like a top, its legs splayed helplessly. A wolf reaches the ice pan and hears the soft whinny of the doomed stallion just ahead. It attacks and the second horse dies.

For an instant the storm lifts revealing a dark line of heavy shrubs only a few meters ahead of the herd. The front horses hesitate seeing the trap but there is no time or way to retreat. They leap headlong into the drifted wall of snow and willow, instantly sinking to their withers. Horses kick and scramble forward, their forelegs churning vainly into the soft, yielding snow. Their short legs serve only to plough them deeper and deeper into the drifts, sucking them down until they vanish beneath the snow. A stallion swings back onto the plain in a desperate bid to escape. The dark shapes of the wolves appear from out of the snowstorm. Two wolves slam into the stallion driving it off its feet into the snow-choked bushes. It staggers and tumbles over backwards, kicking at the attackers. It crumples under the two wolves and is quickly killed.

A wolf leaps into a deep drift where three horses have collapsed on each other. It kills the two floundering on the surface, and then it drives its head deep under the snow, finding the soft neck of the deepest horse that is struggling to resurface. Another wolf launches onto the back of a horse entangled in the shrubs, and rides it until it can no longer stagger forward. There are many dead or dying horses scattered through the bloodstained drifts. A few stallions have escaped by retreating back onto the plain. The small band disappears into the darkening snow squalls on the horizon. The wolf pack is spread out along the edge of the plain, quietly feeding.

The storm has long passed when the moon rises above the north horizon. Two well-fed yearling wolves start to howl in unison. After a few minutes they leave the kills and head out onto the plain. They find a mammoth trail and follow it some kilometers. Suddenly the air is filled with danger. The wolves stand motionless as two dark shapes silently appear from the bushes not far ahead. The lions walk onto the plain towards the wolves, their long tails swinging. Then they roar. The young wolves are rattled and quickly retreat further out on the plain – they are no matches for these great cats. Behind the lions they see a great mammoth carcass, the long white tusks shining in the bright moonlight. A third lion is feeding. It stands and silently watches the wolves pass by. Soon the three cats are all roaring.

The wolves swing far out on the plain and move through a maze of deep drifts back toward the pack. They stumble upon another mammoth carcass and a new, strange smell. They cautiously approach the great body, but are startled by a strange, soft light and cloud of smoke rising from behind the mammoth. They move carefully forward listening to the unfamiliar, muffled sounds coming from the jumble of glowing skins. The wolves silently circle this smoking beast. Suddenly the hide opens and a dark shape walks out on the tundra. It is covered in skins and walks upright like a bear. Its head is covered in long dark hair. Having never before seen this thing the wolves melt back a few meters out of sight.

The man moves to a high pile of snow and digs out a piece of meat, then disappears back under the skins. There is a sharp chorus of noises followed by silence. The wolves retreat behind the mammoth carcass. They slip under the wide ribs and begin to chew half-heartedly at the emaciated torso. A wolf tugs at the exposed and frozen gut hauling out thick strips of empty intestine. There is no fat anywhere and the wolves soon lose interest. They leave and head back through the deep snow toward their pack mates. Soon they are near the horse kills. They raise their heads and howl then stop to listen for a reply.

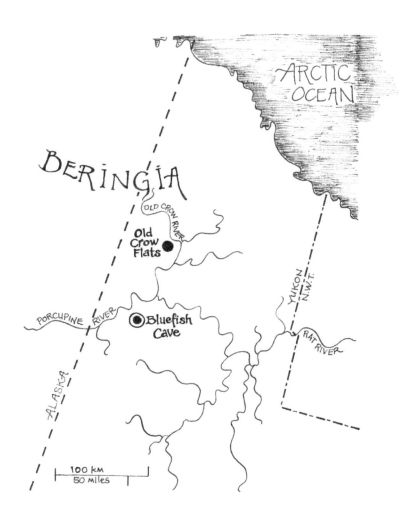

B etween 12,000 and 6,000 years ago the world lost ninety-seven genera of mammals. It was the greatest extinction of mammals ever known. In these few thousand years that mark the transition from the Pleistocene to the Holocene, six Beringia herbivores went extinct: the woolly mammoth, giant ground sloth, giant beaver, giant moose, steppe bison, and horse. Two important predators – the Beringia lion and scimitar cat – also disappeared. As the biodiversity of mammal life collapsed, the first humans arrived in Beringia.

The first signs of human activity found in Beringia were discovered in the Bluefish Caves south of Old Crow Flats in the northern Yukon. There is some evidence that people might have lived here as far back as 24,000 years ago, but there are undisputable human artifacts beginning about 12,000 years ago. There has been a long debate about the impact of human hunting on mammal populations by these first stone-age hunters. One school of thought says Clovis people from southern areas of North America were such good hunters they wiped out the steppe mammals. Others have challenged this overkill theory, claiming the extinctions were caused by the rapid disappearance of grasslands – the critical habitat for the doomed grazers. Recent research by Alaskan paleontologist, Dale Guthrie, shows keystone species like the steppe bison were already declining well before people arrived in Beringia. It seems that humans had little to do with the decline of the mammoth steppe fauna. Instead, ancient nomadic people came into Alaska and the Yukon right at the time when the many species of grazers were already in decline as the steppe grasslands disappeared under shrubs and forests during the Pleistocene-Holocene transition.

About 14,000 years ago the world entered its fourth major interglacial period. For the first time in more than 200,000 years the continental ice sheets began to rapidly melt. As the ice melted the Bering Sea rose, flooding the vast continental shelf grasslands between North America and Asia. Then the climate of Beringia warmed between 13,500 and

11,500 years ago causing a shift away from dry steppe grasslands to shrubs. As the year-round climate moderated more rain and snow fell on the ever-shrinking mammoth steppe. First, birch and willow shrubs rooted in the earth eventually choking out the grasses. Poplar and spruce trees that were long tucked away in isolated places in Beringia found the right environmental conditions to colonize and forests began to take over the lowlands. The mammoth steppe was passing through the eye of a needle and there was something completely different on the other side. The days of grazers were numbered – and the first ones to go were horse and woolly mammoth.

Mammoths and horses were unique because they had a special type of stomach that enabled them to process large amounts of low quality grasses during the Beringia winter when the nutrition quality was mostly leached out of the dead grasses. These two specialized grazers disappeared along with the winter grasses they needed to survive. As the steppe vanished, the horses and mammoths were driven to smaller and smaller ranges until there was simply not enough hay to go around. Wooly mammoths and horses last roamed interior Alaska until about 7,000 years ago, then they both disappear from the fossil record.

As the herds of mammoth and horses collapsed the steppe bison, whose population had long been in decline, suddenly resurged. Able to feed on both grasses and shrubs, steppe bison were common for a few thousand more years, but went extinct about 9,000 years ago and were replaced by a new species, the wood bison.

As the North American ice sheets disappeared life again could move freely across the continent. With the eruption of shrubs and trees the leaf eaters, or browsers, came north. Elk became common throughout the Yukon sometime between 13,000 and 12,000 years ago. Moose arrived about the same time and eventually became the most important browser in the area to this day. The only grazing herbivores to survive the Pleistocene-Holocene shift were caribou, muskox and Dall's sheep. The surviving carnivores were the grizzly bear, the wolverine, and black bear. But did I accurately re-create the wolf in the previous chapter? Did it survive and is the Beringia wolf the ancient ancestor of present day Yukon wolves?

To find the answer we need to first understand how wolves would have fared as the great herds of herbivores vanished around them. The fossil record of the mammoth steppe is well preserved in the Old Crow Flats in the far north Yukon, the scene of this chapter's narrative. It is a place I know well, and a good place to imagine what changes wolves faced at the end of the Pleistocene.

Before I studied wolves, I worked as a waterfowl biologist on the Old Crow Flats, one of the great Arctic wetlands in the world. It was during this time I first became intrigued with the abundant Pleistocene fossils buried in the permafrost under the Flats. In June 1979, I traveled up the Crow River in a boat with my wife Caroline and two young daughters. We pulled off the river at a place named site CRH Locality 11A – a rather uninteresting name for a truly wonderful place. The abandoned beach we stood on was once a bustling study area for many paleontologists in the 1970s.

At first glance 11A looks like the hundreds of beaches that line the winding Old Crow River. But in less than an hour we had combed the sand and assembled a meter high monument of ancient bones: dozens of beautifully preserved horse hooves; a large piece of mammoth molar; various steppe bison, horse and woolly mammoth vertebrae; and shattered ribs and long bones from unknown, long extinct mammals. How the bones ended up on the beach is worth exploring because the prehistory of the Old Crow Basin is an epic tale of environmental change that helps reconstruct and understand what happened in the Yukon at the end of the ice age.

For most of the Pleistocene, the massive Laurentide ice sheet blocked the Porcupine and the Peel Rivers from draining east to the Mackenzie River. With nowhere for the water to go Old Crow Lake slowly flooded the Porcupine River basin and Lake Hughes filled the lower reaches of the Peel River watershed. About 18,000 years ago, Lake Hughes rose high enough to cut a new spillway, instantly draining huge amounts of freshwater northward into the Porcupine River. Old Crow Lake rose until water began to spill out to the west, cutting through a series of rocky ramparts. The Porcupine River began flowing west into the Yukon River system draining Old Crow Lake away about 14,000 years ago. Today all that remains are thousands of small, shallow lakes that have since formed by the melting of permafrost. Each summer ancient bones that are buried in the frozen ground erode out from the bluffs along the Old Crow River. The river floods each spring dumping a fresh supply of ancient bones onto beach 11A – a constant reminder of the fantastic assemblage of mammals that roamed the basin until the end of the Pleistocene.

Today, wolves roaming the Crow Flats eke out a much tougher existence than the horse-hunting wolves of the narrative. During winter there are few moose scattered among the stunted trees and the frozen lakes, browsing on the thin supply of willow bushes buried in the snow. Moose are at the north limit of their continental range, and the low quality of Arctic food keeps their numbers low. Old Crow wolves actually have a tough time finding enough moose to hunt. Packs are small – a result of low pup survival and high mortality of adults. Life is hard for these Arctic wolves – especially if the Porcupine caribou herd winters elsewhere. How would life for Old Crow wolves today compare with the end of the Pleistocene?

In Chapter One we discovered that the wolf was the most successful carnivore of the Pleistocene. They were present during the constant ebb and flow of herbivore species to the very end – the decline in mammoths and horses, followed by steppe bison, then the rapid eruption in elk, moose, and wood bison in the early Holocene. Surely the Beringia wolf survived through the Holocene because it was so good at adapting to changing prey. Ever resourceful, modern wolves feed on human garbage in Italy and Romania. They prey on domestic sheep in France, they kill red deer in Croatia, moose and reindeer in Scandinavia, deer in Minnesota, Peary caribou in Arctic Canada, roe deer in Germany, wood bison in Alberta, and horses and wild asses in Asia. And the list could go on. If there is a way to make a living the wolf can find it. But a recent study says the Beringia wolf could not make the shift into the Holocene.

In 2007 a genetics paper in *Current Biology* concluded Beringia wolves are unrelated to modern Yukon and Alaska wolves. Jennifer Leonard from the University of California and her colleagues examined gene markers and skull measurements of Pleistocene and modern wolves from Alaska. Leonard's discovery was a surprise to wolf biologists – including me. Pleistocene wolves were about the same size as modern ones, but they had a broad mouth palate, more broken and heavily worn teeth, and a specialized large shearing molar. From this skull evidence, Leonard's team concluded the Beringia wolf was a specialist that preferred to handle really big animals, including woolly mammoth, mastodon and steppe bison. But more to the evolutionary point – there are no genetic markers in Beringia wolf skulls that are found in North American wolves. Beringia wolves are related only to Asian wolves according to genes. Leonard's surprising conclusion was the ancestors of the Yukon-Alaska wolf traveled from southern parts of North America sometime in the late Holocene.

When I first read the newspaper reports of this extinct Beringia wolf I was skeptical. Actually, I refused to believe it. What about caribou the great surviving herbivore of Beringia? Surely, I thought, wolves only had to switch to caribou when the other grazers declined. Isotope studies show wolves consumed caribou throughout the Pleistocene so it should have been easy. Caribou became the most common herbivore of the early Holocene. So how could Beringia wolves just up and disappear off the face of the earth? My skepticism hardened but was quickly tempered by Grant Zazula, Yukon paleontologist, who read over early drafts of this book. He explained rather dryly, "Bob, genetics doesn't lie – get over it."

Dale Guthrie is recognized as the world expert of Beringia ecology. When he was asked about this new 'bone-crushing' wolf he said, "It's very interesting and brings to mind the dire wolf." This extinct North American cousin of the gray wolf ranged south of the continental ice sheets during the Pleistocene. The dire wolf disappeared about 10,000 years ago, a victim of being too much scavenger and too little hunter.

It also had a larger head than the gray wolf, and had a dental pattern suited for bone crushing. It seems the genetic evidence shows the Beringia wolf followed the fate of the dire wolf – evolving traits that were narrowly adapted for scavenging from large, doomed steppe herbivores like bison, mastodons and mammoths.

There are other reasons besides genetics that support the idea that the Beringia wolf vanished. Wolf fossils in the Yukon are fairly common from the early Pleistocene, but they steadily decline until they are rare or absent by the early Holocene. The Beringia wolf could have followed the steppe bison, woolly mammoth, horse, and other large herbivores to extinction. Two other predators that lived only in Beringia – the lion and giant short-faced bear – disappeared after the ice age ended so why not the Beringia wolf?

Leonard's genetic and skull evidence describes a unique, and ultimately doomed cousin of the gray wolf living in Beringia. It had bigger teeth and wider palate than the contemporary timber wolf, and it was particularly suited for breaking big bones apart. As mammoth and bison disappeared a robust set of teeth failed to help the wolf through the transition to the Holocene. At the same time, I wonder if we have dug up enough fossils to paint a full and clear picture of the presence of wolves in Beringia. Are there still-buried skulls somewhere in the Yukon that share genes with modern Yukon wolves? I suppose time will tell, and it matters little because the wolf somehow emerges again in the mid Holocene. Caribou were the dominant herbivore, but moose, elk and wood bison erupted as shrubs and forests colonized the Yukon plateaus and valleys. The Yukon wolf faced a new efficient and dangerous competitor for these herbivores.

3

Udzi

Rose Creek - 7,000 years ago

I t is late evening. The June sun is high above the brightly lit mountains on the horizon. Two yearling wolves, a black female and gray male, cast long shadows as they walk briskly through the high shrubs just below the open alpine. The two are following a long sloping ridge leading to a large snow patch perched near the top of a wide plateau. The ridge is carpeted with heather and Arctic willow, the new catkins glistening in the evening sun. Yellow and purple saxifrage flowers and the white petals of the bursting mountain avens are scattered through the dark boulders and black gravel. A vigilant ground squirrel chirps a warning to others as it escapes into its burrow ahead of the wolves. The wolves enter a broad stand of low birch that is about to leaf out. There are large patches of melting snow scattered along the mountainside. The subalpine shrubs are filled with Brewer's sparrow singing their plaintive, high octave territorial song.

The wolves startle a large brood of ptarmigan hidden in the bushes. The covey explodes a few meters away, the young ones pumping their short wings, barely able to fly. The female wolf instinctively jumps over the low shrubs snatching a chick tangled in the branches. With one in her jaws, she tries for a second. But before she can pounce, the second chick is sailing safely down the mountain with the rest of the flock. She downs her prize in a single biting gulp then heads back to the ridge. The male is now far ahead, uninterested in his companion's hunting.

At the end of the ridge the male stops and stands motionless. The evening air is suddenly rich with the smell of prey. The female catches up and the two are soon moving up a wide snow patch. A group of caribou is above them, crowded together on the cooling patch of snow. The wolves separate and walk carefully to avoid exciting the prey. A cow near the bottom of the group is the first to see the two shapes approaching from below. She scrambles to her feet, uncertain of the intentions of the animals that are now coming across the snow. She recognizes the low shapes and their fluid cadence. She knows it is wolves and danger coming. The cow stands and stares at the two wolves for some time then swings quickly up the snowfield with her newborn calf walking briskly by her flank. Now all the caribou are standing looking for the cause of the disturbance. Soon they are all milling together moving slowly uphill, ever watchful of the wolves below. Suddenly they are running, kicking thick slabs of wet snow into the air in their panic to escape.

The female attacks first, heading straight for the large

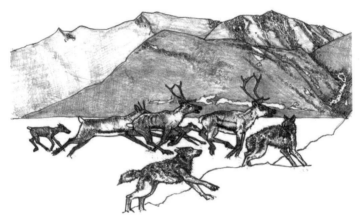

group. The male cuts across the snow following a few animals that are running downhill. His wide paws hold him from slipping in the wet snow and he is quickly among a dozen animals. He pays no attention to the adults. He is after the little ones that are madly running to keep up to their mothers. The week-old calves are fast but no match for him on the snow. In a matter of seconds he kills four of them, fracturing and crushing each tiny skull with a single bite. He stops and glances uphill just in time to see the female disappear over the ridge above. The male walks back to a calf sprawled in the wet snow. With his teeth he snips open its tiny gut then carefully punctures into the warm stomach. He licks the white milk curds that spill forth. When he is done eating the curds, he abandons the carcass and moves to the others and does the same. He lies down on the cool snow and falls asleep.

When he wakes the sun has set. He wanders slowly up the snowfield sniffing at the mounds of caribou dung scattered everywhere. Reaching the top, he spots a group of caribou standing on a distant ridge. He scans the plateau and finds the female sleeping a few hundred meters ahead on a small knoll. She has killed a cow in a field of heather. The male approaches the kill, attracted by the aroma of blood and offal. He moves in carefully, checking her reaction. The male begins to lick at the dark blood pooled inside the carcass. She looks up briefly, then curls up and falls back to sleep. A soft twilight glows on the mountain slopes through the early summer night.

By morning two ravens have found the carcass. They silently circle high above the sleeping wolves. Then a different, new sound startles the wolves awake. A group of humans are moving down a mountain ridge toward the snowfield. The wolves silently watch the approaching group then they move down the snow. A human reaches the carcass first and begins to butcher the caribou. Another man cups his hands to his mouth and mimics a long wolf howl. The wolves turn to look back uphill. Hidden above the ridge, a third man is crawling toward the wolves. He slips a long spear into a notch in a wooden board. He runs in a crouch then he is upright, his weapon held high above him. He drops his shoulder and skips ahead launching the projectile at the wolves. The deadly arrow narrowly misses the female and sails harmlessly onto the snow below them. The wolves run down the snowfield and disappear over a steep grassy ridge. They continue to run until they meet a group of wood bison feeding in the birch shrubs near the bottom of the mountain. A large bull turns and walks casually forward, its sharp dark horns flashing in the early morning sun. The wolves swing away and continue toward home.

Soon they are walking along the valley floor through small stands of spruce and poplars, skirting a series of small pothole lakes. Nearing the den, the male stops on a low ridge and howls for a few minutes. Two pups scramble out of the hole to meet the returning wolves. The female reaches the den first. She slips by the pups and collapses behind a high bush. The pups find her and begin to lick at her mouth searching for food. The male finds his favorite resting place tucked under the low branches of a spruce tree. A third pup scrambles from the den. It climbs to his neck and bites playfully at his ear. He rolls the tiny pup softly in his mouth and growls affectionately.

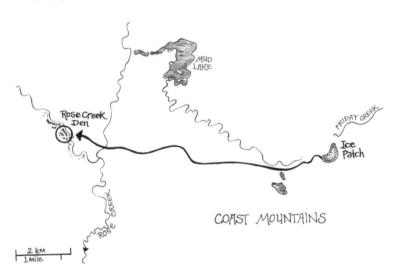

Rose Creek is a high subalpine valley in the southern Yukon full of low shrubs and wet tundra, with thinly scattered spruce on the well-drained lower slopes. At the east end of the valley just to the west of Fish Lake is a large complex of remnant glacial eskers, moraines, and large erratics left behind by the retreating Cordilleran ice. In the centre of the valley, a wolf den sits on a sandy escarpment a few meters above a willow-choked complex of small wetlands. This mountain landscape has hardly changed since the early Holocene. It is still caribou country.

I studied wolves here in the 1980s, my first project as the Yukon's wolf biologist. The Rose Creek pack roamed these mountains hunting moose, caribou and Dall's sheep. In 1982 moose were plentiful and so were wolves. One afternoon in October I watched seventy-five moose move single file along a mountain ridge, high above the wolf den. Today, moose are nearly gone, victims of improved snow-machine technology over the decades and unrestricted hunting by native people. Wolves have also declined sharply, a casualty of the moose disappearance. But over the years I watched the pack raise several litters at the Rose Creek den. The playful wolf behavior at the end of the narrative is another memorable wildlife observation I have had the pleasure to witness.

One day in June, I was lying fifty meters from the den with Jeff Turner, a filmmaker who was making a documentary on wolves. We had flown to Rose Creek in a helicopter, set up a camp, then walked to the den and found a good location to film from without disturbing the wolves. Within minutes Jeff had trained his camera on the alpha female suckling her pups in full view outside the entrance. After some time the female left the area after sending her pups scrambling into the safety of the den. We stayed trained on the den for a long time, until we heard a wolf howling from a high ridge above the valley. We eventually spotted the wolf working its way down the mountain through high shrubs. Jeff swung his camera on the wolf and began filming. As the wolf arrived, a pup scrambled from the den and ran to it. The pup climbed onto the laying wolf and began nipping and pulling at its shoulder with tiny canines. Soon the two were wresting and playing together. All the while the sun was setting, backlighting the scene and forming a shimmering halo around the two wolves. But Jeff's camera began making a clicking sound that could only mean trouble. The scene was never captured on film but my memory of it is there.

The caribou calf-killing event on the ice patch is based on real sightings by other biologists. In one written report a young Arctic wolf chased down and killed some newborn calves, lapping up only the milk curds before wandering off and leaving the tiny carcasses otherwise untouched. Craig Gardner, a biologist in Alaska, watched wolves kill more than a dozen calves in a single evening hunt. Caribou were the primary prey of Yukon wolves during much of the Holocene. As we shall see, the changing Yukon environment was the right place for caribou and for wolves.

By about 10,000 years ago – the date considered to be the start of the Holocene – the Yukon was completely ice free. In the Yukon and Alaska, the warmest period of the Holocene was between 11,000 and 9,000 years ago. As the climate warmed rainfall increased. Shrubs developed then spruce, poplar and birch trees colonized the landscape. In the poorly drained areas willow and dwarf birch replaced the sedge meadows. Today, all that remains of the fabled mammoth steppe are the grass-sage meadows on the south slopes of the mountains. Most of the grassland herbivores have long since disappeared.

Caribou and Dall's sheep are the only surviving grazers of the mammoth steppe. Ten thousand years ago the wolf, wolverine, black and grizzly bear were the only carnivores roaming the rapidly changing landscape. Elk and moose that originally came from Asia in the Pleistocene soon spread, and other mammals soon populated the ice-free Yukon: the wood bison, mountain goat, mule deer and white-tailed deer. Wood bison were present until a few hundred years ago, and then they disappeared. Elk eventually vanished a few thousand years ago. Mountain goat and both species of deer still range in the Yukon but only in isolated areas and in small numbers.

For thousands of years wolves chased, killed and scavenged caribou, bison, and mountain sheep on the mammoth steppe. This long-standing relation shaped how each herbivore foraged, moved, calved, wintered, and generally avoided being killed. This close evolutionary bond is still strong even today, so much so that wolves remain the primary natural force holding both caribou and moose at low abundance in the Yukon.

There is compelling new evidence that caribou ruled the Yukon for much of the Holocene. In 1997, Gerry and Kirsten Kuzyk were hunting sheep in the mountains west of Whitehorse. They came upon a large alpine snow patch that would become one of the most important sites for Holocene paleontologists for the next decade. From the base of the melting ice patch oozed literally tons of soupy, black caribou dung. Gerry was a caribou biologist with the Yukon government and he knew he had found something special.

Caribou had vanished from these southern mountains more than a hundred years ago. The dung had to be old, even ancient. He returned with his boss, Rick Farnell, the Yukon caribou biologist. They collected a handful of feces that turned out to be about 7,000 years old. How did this huge amount of ancient caribou feces end up on top of a mountain? And what could it reveal about the Yukon Holocene? As it turns out the dung would reveal much about the environment of the Yukon for the past 8,000 years. And the ice was also about to reveal incredible details about the ancient people who lived here then.

Caribou move to high mountain snow patches during summer for one reason – to escape the torment by mosquitoes and other biting flies. The dung was produced by thousands of generations of caribou that used the same ice-patch for insect relief. The temperatures in the 1990s were exceptionally warm – enough to melt the deepest layers of ice for the first time since about 8,000 years ago when the Yukon was at the warmest it has been since the Pleistocene. Gerry Kuzyk and Rick Farnell surveyed the mountains of the south Yukon and found a dozen or more similar ice patches in the same state of decay.

Paleontologists scrambled to study the melting ice patches. Suspended in ice for thousands of years the dung contained thawing plant fragments and pollen that revealed exceptional detail about the Holocene landscape. Spruce trees, birch, willow, sedges, horsetail, and sage were the dominant vegetation as far back as 8,000 years ago. Pine pollen appears about 2,000 years ago in the ice. Caribou dung is mixed through all the ice layers showing an unbroken presence for nearly 8,000 years. Wood bison shows up for the first time around 7,500 years ago. Moose, elk, Dall's sheep, and mountain goat appear about 5,000 years ago. But there were other interesting things in the ice.

Scattered through the ice patches were weapons so well preserved they look as if they were just dropped by some careless hunter yesterday. Researchers collected intact spear shafts, a wooden arrow with caribou hair still imbedded in the bone point, and a caribou antler point with brilliant ochre markings. There is even a full bow – ancient hunting tools that previously were only imagined by archaeologists before the ice patch discoveries. The only comparable artifacts are from arid caves in the American southwest. The weapons are significant to the Yukon wolf story because they show that for much of the early Holocene, people relied on caribou for food. All known human sites in the Yukon are associated with caribou areas, and ancient fire pits contain caribou remains – no moose, elk or bison – confirming the reliance on this mountain herbivore. Undoubtedly if people relied on caribou, so would wolves.

If their food moves then wolves will follow. Early Holocene wolf packs probably followed caribou year-round. Caribou were the keystone Holocene species for wolves, but as the climate warmed, shrubs and forest invaded the Yukon paving the way for herbivores that browsed on leaves. First elk then moose moved from southern areas to the expanding forests. Caribou filled the mountains and tundra landscapes of the far north Yukon. As the Holocene climate warmed, wildfires increased. Forest conditions allowed moose to prosper from the mix of climax spruce forests scattered with willows and aspen that grew after wildfire burns. Wolves shifted behaviors to also hunt the growing populations of moose – a beast about four times larger than caribou. For these caribou wolves, hunting moose required a new predation lifestyle.

Imagine a female wolf leading her family through the Yukon winter landscape of the Holocene. She is adapted for chasing down caribou in the open. As the pack moves through the forest it startles a cow moose that is feeding in the snow-filled willows along the shore of a small lake. It weighs 400 kilograms and is about ten times the size of the average wolf. The wolves have seen these big beasts before, but they have not yet registered them as possible food. The cow moves into a stand of thick spruce trees, firmly placing its hind end under the long branches. As the wolves approach she drops her head and stamps her powerful front legs. There is no way to attack from the rear. Getting between the tree and those hind legs is too dangerous. The female wolf has never tested moose before. She reconsiders and moves off followed by her pack. But her mate remains behind and tries for the cow from the side. The moose shifts sideways to face him. The male runs a few steps in a bluffing attack, still tentative and unsure. With lightning speed the cows kicks its powerful front legs out barely missing the wolf's head by a few centimeters. It is too big and dangerous, and impossible to kill around the trees. This moose is a 'stander', and unless it can be made to run it cannot be killed without high risks. The wolf leaves and catches up to his pack that is already moving out of the willows onto the snowy lake.

A week later the pack passes here again. This time the cow is walking across the lake and everything changes. The lake is windblown and the ice is hard and slick, an impossible place for the moose to stand and defend itself. As the pack surrounds the cow it becomes nervous. The wolves sense this new advantage. The cow's hard hooves have little purchase on ice. Her only escape is to head for the shore. But if she runs she will be exposed for attacks. Before the wolves can move closer the cow makes its last mistake. The cow runs but soon panics as she slips and slides across the smooth ice. Moose have become wolf prey.

I happened upon a wolf pack testing a moose on lake ice near Teslin one winter day. I could see many places where the moose had slipped trying to defend itself along the lake surface. The wolves had not yet wounded the animal, but as I left the area in the plane I thought things would go in the wolves favor. I checked back a few days later to find the dismembered carcass on the lake, the wolves already gone.

Besides the great supply of fresh meat that a moose serves up, there were other advantages for Holocene wolves to begin hunting moose. Instead of following migratory caribou for hundreds of miles each year, moose-hunting wolves did not have to range too far to find prey. As moose became plentiful, Holocene wolves began to establish territories and defend their food supply from other wolf packs. Woodland caribou were distributed everywhere in the Yukon, so by staying in one area, wolves soon learned everything they needed to know about the year-round distribution of both moose and caribou. Wolf body size grew to handle the larger moose prey. Today the Yukon timber wolves are among the largest race of *Canis lupus* in the world – direct ancestors of these highly adaptable predators of the Holocene.

4

The Provider

T he two brothers move silently through the forested ridge above the river. They are each wearing light moccasins, long trousers and fringed over-shirts all made from caribou skins. The oldest boy carries a two-meter bow made of Douglas maple and a quiver of spruce arrows. In his hand he holds an arrow tipped with a carved antler point. A leather sack slung loose over his shoulder slaps lightly against his waist as he runs through the forest.

The June sun is high and the new leaves on the willows below shine bright green in the afternoon light. They are nearing the place and begin to walk quietly, stopping now and then to listen. As the brothers reach the end of the ridge, they scare up a ruffed grouse that flushes from behind a spruce tree a few meters away. They freeze and stand motionless but hear only the small yellow birds singing from the nearby bushes. But then the sound comes – the sound they both were silently hoping they would not hear. The wolves are home. Their simple plan has now turned dangerous.

The howling is coming from the place their father showed them two moons ago when there was snow on the ground. But now their father is far away at their summer fish camp on Kloo Lake. It is the first time they have traveled so far without him and their first time to visit a wolf den. The oldest boy slips the arrow onto his bow and moves down the ridge. His young brother follows a few meters behind. He carries a spear pointed ahead. They are both nervous and frightened, but neither speaks of it.

The mother wolf hears them moving along the ridge and barks out a sharp warning. She knows it is man approaching by the soft sounds on the forest floor. She nudges the pups into the den then slips silently through the bushes toward the coming sound.

The brothers are on their way down the steep ridge when they see the dark shape darting through the willows ahead of them. Then a wolf howls somewhere across the river and another answers from the ridge behind them. The boys stand silently for some time listening to the howling chorus, unsure of what to do.

The younger brother nods in the direction of the den and keeps moving down the ridge. As they near the den, they see many wolf scats that lead to the freshly dug hole nestled among a maze of high shrubs. Hoping there is no adult below, the oldest boy drops onto his stomach and he presses his head into the hole listening for movement inside. He can smell the pups hidden somewhere below.

The younger brother gathers a handful of dry grass and scoops some small branches from the ground with his free hand. He pulls his flint from his waist belt and strikes at it until the grass ignites. Feeding more twigs on the flame he scoops his hands into the soil under the fire cradling the smoldering mass into the den entrance. His brother nods silently, then he stands and turns around slowly, his bow raised to his shoulder. The wolves are howling all around, but none are visible. The boys both crouch at the entrance waiting for pups to emerge. The howls and barks of wolves come closer.

Below, the den chambers fills with a thick, acrid smoke. The pups begin to whine in distress. The first one dashes out from a small side hole beside the main entrance, but the boys see it and catch it easily. It bites at their hands as they stuff it roughly into the sack. Soon they have four pups inside. They have finished their task, and they scramble to their feet to leave.

The mother wolf moves silently though the willows approaching the intruders. She barks sharply and drops her head down. She stares at the two boys growling low and barring her white teeth. The youngest boy snatches a pup from his brother's sack and bowls it on the ground toward its mother. The pup scrambles to its feet and dashes into the bushes behind her. Her hackles raised, she stands and barks frantically.

The boys raise their weapons and move slowly back up the ridge. Watching them, the female moves to the den entrance and stands there rigid and motionless – in close range and a perfect target. The oldest carefully raises his bow until the arrow reaches his eye-level. He pulls slowly on the string arching the bow back. The arrow is sighted on the shoulder of the wolf less than ten meters away. But as he is about to let the arrow loose there is a loud bark to his left. He flinches slightly just as his finger releases the projectile. The arrow passes under the wolf's legs and disappears somewhere behind her. She leaps away and vanishes in the thick bush.

The young boys scramble up the ridge until they reach the top. They stop and check behind expecting to see a dozen wolves at their heels. Wolves are howling and barking from all directions, but there is nothing in sight. The boys turn and race along the ridge for nearly an hour, finally arriving at a broad open meadow. They are exhausted and stop to drink from a small brook winding through the grass. Ground squirrels scold them from the safety of their burrows. The oldest boy swings the sack off his shoulder and carefully opens the top. He pets the pups curled up inside then he shows his brother. The two boys smile then they are off running again, now only a few kilometers to home. As he runs the oldest feels anxious thinking about what he must tell his father. He has lost the antler point his father carved him one long winter evening in the skin house at Aishihik Lake. He must return to the den and search for it when the wolves leave after the summer.

Back at the den the female paces back and forth whining softly. The small fire finally dies and cools. She steps over the glowing embers and slips inside the den. The arrow is buried deep in the den wall blocking her way. She bites it breaking it at the tip then she crawls to the nest chamber. A pup is curled up fast asleep. She lies down beside it but she does not sleep.

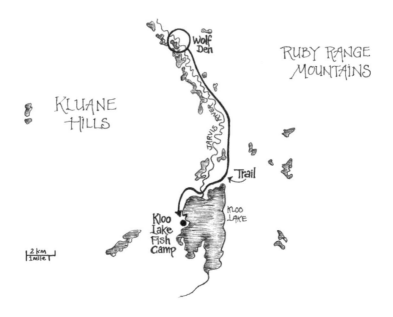

O n 25 May 1995 I circled over the Jarvis River den in a helicopter scanning for the radio signals of the Kloo Lake wolves. I could barely hear the faint signal of the collared adult female in my head set. She was many kilometers away to the north, and not at home. The helicopter dropped onto a marshy meadow beside the river. As we landed I opened the door and checked to make sure the tail rotor was clear of trees. I gave a thumbs-up to the pilot and the Jet Ranger settled noisily on the wet meadow at our destination.

When the blades finally stopped turning I listened carefully for wolves. Dan Drummond, a conservation officer, shuffled out of the backseat. We walked to the den hidden in high bushes ringed by a complex of small ponds. The den site was a series of collapsed mounds, old tunnels and overgrown holes. As I approached I looked for sign that pups had been raised there that summer. But there were no tiny scats and no attending adults –

only silence. As I walked the trails Dan crawled into a freshly excavated hole and disappeared so that only his boot heels were visible. He emerged from the hole grinning and holding up something.

"This thing was buried in the side of the den", he said, handing me the object. It was about ten centimeters long, curved and ornately barbed. I could see that someone had made it with great care and skill. Knowing little about archaeology we speculated it was some kind of spear point made of animal bone, probably used for fishing. Dan placed the prize in his pocket and I did not think about it again until I met Greg Hare, an archeologist for the Yukon government, some years later.

Greg was showing me the fantastic collection of Holocene weaponry in his office. His cabinets contained dozens of artifacts including full size wooden spears, atlatl atlatl projectiles, bows, arrows, and other historical fragments found at alpine ice patch sites in the south Yukon. As I looked over the materials I recognized various antler points that resembled Dan's. I told Greg about our find at the Jarvis River wolf den, and he asked if he could take a small piece to carbon date it. I called Dan and he delivered the antler point to Greg.

I saw Greg months later and he said – rather casually, "You know we carbon dated that point at about 850 years old. It is beautifully preserved." I was astonished and then confused. "I thought something that old would have rotted in the ground." Greg explained that the arrow was well preserved because it was protected inside the den where it was dry and well ventilated. Greg thought someone shot the arrow into the den. I pondered the implications.

The antler point was in the wall of a den complex that had been used for nearly a thousand years by many generations of wolves. Using similar dating methods biologists found a den on Ellesmere Island used by Arctic wolves for over 700 years. The long-term use means the knowledge of these sites was passed down from one wolf generation to the next making these ancient places important ecological areas. I know of a hundred or more wolf dens scattered through the Yukon, and wonder that other ones have also been occupied for hundreds, perhaps even thousands of years.

The beautifully carved arrow point that Dan pulled from the wall of the Jarvis River wolf den is also the first evidence of an ancient human activity – denning, or killing or capture of wolf pups. Native elders have told me about denning for years but I had no idea it went so far back in time. Ancient Yukon native people must have known the locations of many wolf dens. Den sites are traditionally used from year to year and they are often in wildlife-rich wetland areas (see Chapter Thirteen) – the same places that people would go to collect food in summer.

Yukon native elders tell a similar denning story. Dens were raided and pups were taken alive or killed. Usually one pup was spared so the spirit of the wolf is appeased and the person is kept safe from bad luck. Remarkably, the same denning practices occur in Asia. Stockbreeders in Kyrgyzstan take pups from wolf dens leaving one behind, but they go a step further than what I heard from Yukon elders. They sever the tendons of the pup so the spirit of the wolf cannot chase them down. It should be no surprise that the practice of denning is shared in Asia and the Yukon. Most anthropologists believe that the first people in Beringia traveled from Asia over the Bering land bridge at the end of the Pleistocene. The shared practices are compelling because it means the traditional activity was strong enough to stay in use for thousands of years on both continents.

There are good reasons why Yukon native people denned wolf pups. The pups were prized and taken alive to breed with working dogs. Wolf-dog hybrids are known for their strength and endurance, despite their vicious tempers. Jack London's Klondike fiction describes Yukon native people traveling with half-wolf sled dogs that were large, strong and quite dangerous. Interbreeding still continues but is uncommon nowadays.

Another reason Yukon native people took pups was to reduce wolf competition for big game – perhaps the original method of controlling wolf numbers. Elders say that denning happened when caribou herds were low and people feared starvation. The idea of reducing wolves to increase low game populations is still important today among Yukon native people (see Chapter Sixteen) – although I don't know of any native people denning pups except during recent bounty times.

Ron Chambers, a member of the Champagne and Aishihik First Nation, told me denning was also practiced to protect dogs. Yukon native people depended on their dogs for year-round transportation. Pack dogs were used to move families to fishing lakes, summer and winter hunting ranges, and to travel to berry and traditional medicine plant places. Dogs were packed with dried fish and meat and used to fill winter caches. In winter, dog teams pulled sleds of hunters and trappers. Without dogs, the nomadic life was not possible. There are plenty of stories of wolves raiding camps at night and killing dogs – so the fear of losing dogs was real. Native people would have made great efforts to protect their primary method of transport. Without dogs there was a real chance people could starve. But the wolf was also seen as a provider in times of starvation.

Ethnologist Catherine McLellan wrote two fine books about Yukon native people. *Part of the Land, Part of the Water* is the history of Yukon native peoples and *My Old People Say* is a collection of traditional stories that reveal the spiritual beliefs and mythology about the important animal world. The books contain stories that reveal how *Udzi*, the wolf, fit into the spiritual, social and cultural fabric of society. Like most animals, wolves were killed and used for subsistence but killed wolves were never eaten. Ancient native people made sinew snares and deadfalls to kill wolves for their fur. Although the fur was valued for trimming clothing, the living wolf was seen to be important as a provider of food in hard times and a spirit of good luck. The strong theme of wolf as the provider of food is recorded in many stories.

The Gwich'in people tell a story that long ago people asked the wolf to help them find caribou. A hunter followed a lone wolf track and when he finally found the wolf it showed him the direction of the caribou by howling. In this way the wolf led the hungry hunter to caribou and food. Native peoples in the south Yukon have similar stories that feature a wolf-human entity that helps people find food in hard times. Tagish First Nation elder Angela Sidney tells how a human and a wolf spirit-helper became a binding force for the person's clan, and how it became the clan crest.

"A man went hunting caribou to save his father's people the Dakl'awei di from starvation. But he was unable to find any caribou. After following caribou tracks a long way the man made camp for the night. He came upon the camp of a strange lone boy with a painted face and a wolf tail tied to his cap. There was a big fire so the man asked to camp with the boy. The boy told the man that he had killed many caribou and he was welcome to take all he wanted. They became friends and boy told the man he is going away to kill more caribou. The boy gave the man his snowshoes, bow and arrows and said, 'you be Wolf. I'm Wolf. I want you to be

Wolf.' In the morning when the man woke the strange boy was gone and there was no fire or camp. A wolf bed was all that remained. The man returned home with a great supply of caribou. He told his wife, 'I got good luck.' He told her about the boy and showed her the snowshoes and bow and arrow. He told her the boy said, 'From now on you are going to be lucky.' That's how come Dakl'awei di own Wolf. My father's people, they own Wolf."

The Teslin-Tlingit First Nation people tell a story of a wolf-man called *Caribou Killer* who took a human form and killed caribou for a starving old man. He then spent the night in camp with the old man but went away crying when the man accidentally burnt his arrows in the fire. This myth explains why there are tear marks down the cheek of a wolf skin. Like the previous story the wolf-man gives the old man the caribou he killed, "I don't want them. You'll see me again. Remember that my tears have ended just above my cheek-bone." In honor of wolf, the modern chief of the Teslin Tlingit First Nation still ties a black handkerchief around his head the same way *Caribou Killer* did, meaning he is the top provider of his people.

The theme of wolf as provider is strong among Yukon native people. These stories evolved from people following wolves or accidentally finding prey carcasses to take needed food from. In this way wolves became revered for their ability to kill big game animals – a powerful skill that people could emulate. To become better runners the faces of young dogs were smeared with wolf fat to increase endurance. A young boy was given fresh wolf skin to eat so he would be long winded. Warriors studied the wolf and used the animal in patterns of war magic. A Southern Tutchone war party preparing to attack an enemy ate raw snowshoe hare emulating the wolf spirit. Victorious warriors howled like wolves by the camp of the defeated.

But Yukon native people also feared wolves and some still do today. They say a wolf can attack people if it is starving – and there are such stories. The Southern Tutchone people tell a story of wolves killing a young girl who was sent off to a bush camp, and another story about an old woman who was killed by wolves when she crossed a lake at night. The Kaska people of the southeast Yukon say wolves 'go crazy with hunter' and will attack people in spring when big game is hard to find. The wolf was viewed as a provider but Yukon native people maintained a healthy respect for the dangerous nature of the predator.

Wolves were also respected for their intelligence and were thought to be as smart as people. Tetlit Gwich'in people believe in reincarnation and say only the wolf, or *zhoh*, is smart enough for a man's soul to enter into. Yukon native people view wolves and bears as their equals. Both animals have special powers, able to hear the thoughts of humans. It is bad luck to say ill things about wolf or bear. When someone kills a wolf, bad luck will follow unless the wolf's spirit is appeased somehow. They cut the sinews of the legs so the animal's spirit is not able to chase them down. Here we find a similar tradition to the Kyrgyz stockbreeders who cut the sinew of pups for the same reason. After shooting a wolf, a hunter wraps its hair around the gun barrel otherwise he might never hit a target again. The Vuntut Gwich'in people will not look a wolf in the eye for fear of bad luck. However, wolves bring good luck for those who treat them properly. When a Gwich'in person dreams about the wolf it is a sign of good luck. Wolves become the protector of the family members who share the same wolf dream.

Making apologies to wolves was taken seriously. The Teslin-Tlingit First Nation people tell a story about a woman who killed a wolf. She was taught to say, "Pity me grandfather. Excuse me for making a mistake. I just killed you by mistake. I am your grandchild." In another story, wolves came into camp after a woman brought a wolf hide inside a cabin. Her mother spoke to the wolves admitting the error.

"She told the wolves that she was sorry and that she would put the skin outside. Then it was just as if one wolf was telling the next, and their voices died out one by one as they sat there in the circle. And then they all went away."

Making apologies to wolf and bear continues to this day. In July 1998, I attended a culture camp for native youth to talk about wolf biology. The speaker before me was instructing the group about bear and wolf safety. He sometimes told jokes and sometimes spoke about wolves and bears in a light, comedic way. When his talk ended I thought he did a good job, and I was at first surprised when a native elder in the audience stood and said he was upset because the speaker was laughing at bears and wolves. He warned the audience that bears and wolves heard everything that was said – and they never forget. Bad luck would happen if we all did not apologize to wolf and bear spirits. I quietly made my apology.

The deep connection of Yukon native people to wolves makes sense as both shared the same nomadic lifestyles. The wolf and prehistoric native peoples lived in similar extended family units moving constantly in search of the moose, caribou, sheep, and other food resources. Because they were often after the same animals, wolves and people must have seen and encountered each other often in the wilderness. People watched wolves hunting and learned how to approach and kill different animals.

By emulating the wolves' strategies people improved their chances of survival. In desperate times wolf-killed carcasses were viewed as gifts from the wolf, further strengthening the spiritual connection.

This intimate relationship between wolves and humans in the Yukon wilderness slowly evolved over thousands of years. Yukon native people shared the landscape with the wolf, developing a dependency on the animal during hard times. The animal became a mythical spirit that needed to be carefully appeased because people were often at risk of starvation, and survival required some luck in a difficult subsistence life. Native peoples also developed a healthy fear of wolves, and were careful not to make the wolf unhappy and tip the delicate balance. But in 1897 everything changed for Yukon native peoples and for the wolf.

5

The Primordial Beast

Yukon River - early December 1897

The wolves watch the long shadow of the first man moving slowly through the thin fog along the edge of the bright moonlit river. He is hauling a large sled. The other humans follow trudging through the snow. The wolves are close enough to hear the shallow breathing of the laboring men. The man in front stops and adjusts his rope harness. He spits loudly; his steamy saliva crackles and freezes before it touches the snow. The others stop among the jumble of river ice chunks. Their breath comes as ice fog, instantly forming a thick veil around them. Heavy, fur-trimmed hoods hide their dark bearded faces. They talk in low voices. Then they return into their harnesses and continue moving upstream on the ice. As they pass by the wolves, man-scent settles through the trees.

The wolves wait hidden on the shore until the men round the river bend and disappear from sight. There is the sound of splashing in water followed by loud shouting. The male wolf cautiously moves onto the open ice and looks upriver past the frozen chaos of broken and twisted ice floes shining in the bright moonlight. He sees the dark forms of men moving into dense trees lining the riverbank.

Suddenly a tree cracks. The sound splits the cold, dense air like a thunderclap. Startled the wolf leaps back into the forest, brushing quickly past his mate and pups. They turn and quietly retreat with him a short distance into the trees. They all stand silently together unsure of where to go. But the female is anxious to travel tonight. She returns back to the river and watches. The male moves slowly back onto the ice and the rest of the pack follows. They walk carefully across the wide river, navigating between the ice floes in a tight single file.

This is the first time the pack will cross the freshly frozen river with the pups. The fast flowing water rumbles beneath the thin ice. Instinctively, the pups step into the tracks of the leading adults, careful to stay on their trail. Their prints are so close together that it appears a single wolf has walked through the jumbled ice blocks.

The pack finally reaches the smooth ice along the opposite bank. The wolves disappear single file into a dense thicket of shrubs lining the shore. But the last pup catches the fleeing shadow of a snowshoe hare bolting for the river. The pup spins in the trail and takes pursuit. The hare is leaping wildly through the ice chunks with the racing pup close behind. With a sudden crack and a splash, the pup is gone.

The alpha female takes the lead and begins to work her way through the deep snow. Soon she is under the cover of trees where the snow is shallow. The pack moves silently upriver until they are directly across from the men busy on the other shore. There is a large fire burning. The shadows of the men dance against the wall of thick green branches. There are sharp sounds and shouts as trees begin to fall.

The two adult wolves slip under the boughs of a large spruce tree. The rest of the pack sense this is as far as they will go tonight. They turn in tight circles preparing their snow beds for sleeping. Soon the wolf family is asleep. The female is woken by the soft sound of voices in the night. She notices the male is no longer in his bed. She stands and with her nose finds his trail heading down to the river. It is only then she senses one of her pups is missing. She heads back through the sleeping wolves checking for its scent. It is not here. She walks back down the trail the way they had come with her nose low in the tracks. She smells all her pups except for one. She reaches the place where the pack left the river. Its scent is here but it is moving to the ice. She follows its tracks out onto the river until it stops at the open water. The mother wolf lets out a long howl.

The male is standing along the river edge listening to the men, drawn by the smell of cooking food. He hears his mate's voice coming from downriver. The pups' high voices reply from the edge of the dark forest behind him. The male moves quickly back and gathers the howling pups together. They move down the trail towards their mother. The male sees the silhouette of his mate, her nose high in the air still howling. Anxious, he looks up the river. The men are standing at the edge of the glowing firelight silently looking toward the wolves.

The pups start to whine and cautiously approach their mother. The male moves close and joins her howling. The pups join in. Suddenly, and as if on cue, the howling ends. There is only the low sound of water racing beneath the ice. The two adults slip back to the forest making a new trail downriver. The fire has been built up and is much brighter now, casting dark shadows on the white ice. A few hundred meters into the forest the pack stops again and listens but there is no sound except for the hoots of a great-horned owl in the distance. The wolves move further into the comfort of the shadowy forest.

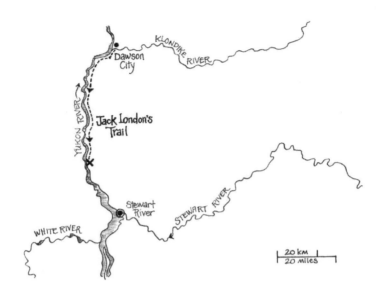

n early December 1897 Jack London, a young adventurer and aspiring writer, traveled up the Yukon River from Dawson City with some companions. He was returning to his gold claim at Stewart City. The temperature had dropped to a bone chilling -67°F. The men had spent the previous six weeks camped near Dawson City staking claims, collecting mail, receiving news from 'outside', checking out the entertainment, and 'generally posting themselves in the country'. London never kept a journal so his time in Dawson City and the events on the frigid walk up river were never recorded, but I can imagine the men might have encountered timber wolves like the ones I have described.

London's best dog-wolf fictions were all set in the Klondike region of the central Yukon. The stories were important not only because they are great entertainment but also because they introduced millions of people around the world to the northern wilderness. After reading *Call of the Wild* or *White Fang*, readers in the early 1900s were left with new perceptions about wilderness and wolves. At the time, London's wolf and half-wolf characters became household names – powerful symbols that would influence how people viewed wolves worldwide. His fiction was the most important early influence of my love of wilderness, and his books kindled my early interest to move to the Yukon to work as a biologist. I never dreamed I would one-day study London's 'primordial beast'.

So how much did Jack London known about wolves and the Yukon wilderness? I expect not much. He spent less than a year in the Klondike never venturing more than a few kilometers from the banks of the Yukon River. He was a reluctant gold miner, hardly turning a shovel. He came north in 1897 with thousands of dreamers that scrambled across the Chilkoot Pass in search of Klondike riches. He staked a gold claim and worked it half-heartedly. During the long, cold winter he contracted scurvy sending him back home to California in the spring of 1898. We will never know whether London even saw or heard a Yukon wolf but the details of his fiction makes me think he must have. He certainly could have heard wolves that winter, and would have listened to many wolf stories – some far fetched – when visiting neighbors in Stewart City. Whatever the case, his brief time in the Yukon provided material for some of the most successful popular fiction written.

London featured dogs and wolves in his best known Klondike fiction in two books: *The Call of the Wild* and *White Fang*. London's canine protagonists were capable of sophisticated human thoughts, emotions and behavior. His dogs were heroic and compassionate, representing the softer, civilized side of life. Wild wolves were the opposite – metaphors of ruthlessness, death and unforgiving wilderness. He called wolves "primordial beasts" – wild animals that survived by instinct alone in a world ruled by a simple law, "Kill or be killed, eat or be eaten." Wolves and their half-wolf cousins always fought to the death – there were no holds barred, no quarter given. They showed no mercy because it had no survival advantage. Killing was the necessary and inevitable solution to live on in the wilderness and, given the right chance, wolves would even kill humans. *White Fang* eventually attains the high emotions of love, compassion, and mercy. But first White Fang suffered great abuse, and then he needed to be tamed before becoming civilized. To his literary critics *White Fang* was a metaphor and London seemed to be saying humans must also eventually tame wilderness.

According to London, he was unaware of any deeper meaning to his dog fiction. When *Call of the Wild* was published critics praised the book calling it a well-crafted fable about the conflict between civilization and wilderness told through the actions and thoughts of Buck, London's most famous canid protagonist. London replied the book was merely a lucky piece of writing and he intended no more than a good read. Conscious or not, symbols run deeply through London's fiction.

Taking his writing as a form of allegory, London is telling us we are drawn to wilderness because we need it to challenge us from time to time. The primal experience makes us stronger and better suited to succeed in our own society. To become heroic is good, because it means success. Wolves are the animation of the unknown wilderness because they have no compassion for weakness. A passage from *White Fang* describes the dogs' fear of the wolf character:

"He was the wild – the unknown, the terrible, the ever-menacing, the thing that prowled in the darkness around the fires of the primeval world where they (dogs), cowering close to the fires, were reshaping their instincts, leaving to fear the wild out of which they came, and which they had deserted and betrayed."

Through simple but elegant prose, London suggests that wolves are the antithesis of civilization. To follow the wolf's wild ways we are "...going back into the womb of Time," where the hunt and day-to-day survival are all there is, all that is truly important.

London's heroic dog stories include impossible journeys of extreme hardship filled with abuse and hatred often inflicted by bad men. Evil behavior is reserved for dogs or dog-wolf crosses that were abused by the hand of man. Wild wolves, on the other hand, kill only to survive and never out of malice.

London's wolves also represent a human need for a purely visceral and heroic connection to nature, a theme that emerged in much of the hunting literature at the turn of the century. Like Theodore Roosevelt, London was fascinated by man's primal attraction for leaving the comforts of civilization to chase and hunt wild animals for sport. London's wolves represented the purest hunter. In the final chapters of *The Call of the Wild*, Buck takes longer and longer hunting sorties away from cabin life, drawn further into the forest by a primitive magnetism:

"The blood-longing became stronger than ever before. He was a killer, a thing that preyed, living on the things that lived, unaided, alone, by virtue of his own strength and prowess, surviving triumphantly in a hostile environment where only the strong survived. Because of all of this he became possessed of a great pride in himself, which communicated itself like a contagion to his physical being."

London seems to be saying an ethical, honest hunter is worthy of the highest respect from society.

When we look for the truths and myths about wolves in his fiction, we have to give London his due for choosing entertainment over accurate biology. The first chapters of *White Fang* are high entertainment because the writing is so good and the wolf biology is so far-fetched. The story begins with two men driving a dog team through the forest carrying a coffin containing a dead man over a frozen winter trail. They are attacked by a great pack of forty starving wolves led by a cunning wolf-dog hybrid that lures the sled dogs away one by one to their grisly deaths. Then the wolves attack and kill the two desperate men who are running low in ammunition. There is a little truth and a lot of fiction here. There are plenty of accounts of wolves snapping dogs from chains behind a cabin, and this still happens regularly in the Yukon. But there has not been a person killed by wolves in the Yukon in living memory. A woman I know was chased by a lone wolf and was able to avoid it by circling a large rock. In the end, the wolf appeared to be interested in the dog with her, but the likelihood the wolf was after her cannot be dismissed either.

Imagine London submitting the *White Fang* manuscript to a more factually correct publisher today. We would certainly have a less exciting yarn. London's mega pack of forty starving wolves would be much smaller if the biology was accurate. When food is scarce, wolf packs disintegrate into small groups or they hunt alone. If food is short, large packs cannot feed all the wolves. Wolves can search more places for prey by splitting up. Small packs also reduce the chance of wolves killing each other over disputed food, a common cause of mortality even among well-fed wolves. The biologically correct *White Fang* would dispose of the cunning dog-wolf hybrid leading the attack. A hybrid does not know the complex social behavior required to survive let alone lead scores of wild cousins. At best, the new story line would have a few starving wolves follow the men for a short time, kill a couple of dogs at night while the men slept, then head off in search of less dangerous prey. It is a more accurate but infinitely less exciting read.

The same editor would question London's attempt to make a wolf out of Buck, the giant St. Bernard-husky cross in *The Call of the Wild*. There are important behaviors for Buck to overcome before he could become a member of a wolf pack, let alone a leader. Buck was a domestic dog. Buck would never have figured out the complex sociology of a wild pack before the wolves turned on him and killed him.

Buck's other problems were physical. Weighing nearly seventy kilograms, he was considerably heavier than the average wolf. Wolves walk most waking hours of their life. They have evolved large, broad feet that keep them from sinking deep in snow. They are also narrow framed with long legs that efficiently slip behind one another when they travel, reducing snow drag and minimizing energy loss. Buck's huge size and short legs would not have kept him from sinking deep in the snow, and his gait would have been entirely inefficient. Buck would have been exhausted after a few kilometers stumbling and pushing his large body along the wolf trail. After the first day he would be left far behind the pack to starve. Pulling down moose or caribou in the winter would be impossibly difficult. Buck might have survived his first winter in the Yukon wilderness only if he stumbled onto a human to befriend and feed him. That's the biological reality.

But London did get some of his wolf biology right. His description of Buck killing a wounded bull moose is believable. I have seen a few lone wolves harass moose for many days before fatally wounding them. But Buck figures out how to do this by apprenticing for a few short weeks killing squirrels. A wolf learns how to kill by watching its parents hunt many big game animals. Before it is two years old and ready to leave home, it has had a front seat view of more than a hundred moose kills. This ground training is critical to prepare a wolf for the harsh carnivore life. With no training, my guess is Buck would have been kicked to death by the moose, or he would have thought better of it and returned to the squirrels.

London's description of White Fang's life as a newborn pup is good and so is the chronology of his development at the den. He loses his littermates to famine shortly after birth. London was also right to link the starvation of the pups to the death of White Fang's father. A mother wolf depends on her mate for nourishment and milk production when she is den-bound. If her mate dies the pups will probably starve to death. Nearly eighty percent of Yukon wolf pups die in their first year of life to famine, accidents, predation, and other causes.

Today, thanks to writers like London, we see wolves as the embodiment of complete wilderness. Without wolves there is a missing element of wilderness that keeps wild populations in check, and holds the natural ecosystem in a dynamic balance. A good example was the move to reintroduce wolves to Yellowstone National Park in the western United States in the mid 1990s. Without wolves, Yellowstone – for many people – was incomplete. London's Klondike fiction sowed the first seeds that the wolf had an essential role in how true wilderness functions.

Robert Service was nearly as influential as London at using the wolf as an allegory of wilderness. Service wrote some of the most popular poems in the English language. And like Jack London, he lived in the Yukon during the Klondike gold rush. Service's *The Land God Forgot* is one of the most inspiring wilderness poems I know. It was my mother's favorite poem. The poetry evokes beauty, dread and desperation of a land sinking into winter darkness – robbing any chance of hope. In the last two stanzas Service introduces the wolf as the metaphor for the coming loneliness and despair.

> So gaunt against the gibbous moon,
> piercing the silence velvet-piled,
> a lone wolf howls his ancient rune,
> the fell arch-spirit of the Wild.
> O outcast land! O leper land!
> Let the lone wolf-cry all express
> the hate insensate of thy hand,
> thy heart's abysmal loneliness.

The wolf howling embodies the terror of the coming winter night. Only someone who has witnessed the fading sun on the horizon at the end of a light-starved Yukon December day could write this wonderful poem. Although Service never wrote a poem specifically about wolves his sparse use of the wolf is scattered through his best poetry. In *The Law of the Yukon* Service uses the wolf as a parable for how the trials of a wilderness life will crush the weak hearted:

> Staggering blind through the storm-whirl,
> stumbling mad through the snow,
> frozen stiff in the ice-pack,
> brittle and bent like a bow;
> featureless, formless, forsaken,

scented by wolves in their flight,

left for the wind to make music,

through ribs that are glittering white;

gnawing the black crust of failure,

searching the pit of despair,

crooking the toe in the trigger,

trying to patter a prayer.

The Heart of the Sourdough is Service's ode to the Cheechako, the men and women who lived through their first Yukon winter. It is defiant and heroic poetry but fatalistic. Men might find temporary victory but wilderness will always win – defeating even the strongest ones. Again, the poem has the wolf as wilderness symbol. The first lines establish the life-death struggle:

There, where the mighty mountains bare

their fangs unto the moon.

The poem then celebrates our need for wilderness, and our inevitable failure to survive there:

Then when, as wolf-dogs fight, we've fought,

the lean wolf-land and I;

fought and bled till the snows are red

under the reeling sky;

even as lean wolf-dogs go down

will I go down and die.

Thanks to Robert Service and Jack London, the Yukon has become a mythical wilderness and the wolf has become its animated character or symbol. Both independently invented the wolf as an enduring allegory for a harsh and unforgiving land that is as dangerous as it is beautiful. To millions of readers and armchair adventurers around the world, the mythical connection between wolves and the Yukon endured and grew so that today tourists come to the territory to experience its wild outdoors. London's stories and Service's poetry inspire a desire to travel to the Yukon. Many Europeans come to feel a wilderness that disappeared in their own countries centuries ago. Knowing the wolf shares the same wilderness spaces is an essential part of many Yukon tourists' seminal experience. It is also why I moved to the Yukon and why people still come here to live.

But to most of the people that came to the Yukon in the early 1900s looking for their fortune, the wolf was just another wild animal to be hunted or trapped for its fur. The men and women who stayed after the Klondike gold rush spread through the territory. They built cabins, worked odd jobs, hunted big game, fished, cut wood, and trapped for a living. A prime winter wolf pelt was useful for parka trim and other outdoor clothing. This simple subsistence view of the wolf was about to change as the world began to prepare for the First World War. Wolves in many wilderness areas of North America were unknowingly on the brink of their own great battle. After the Klondike gold rush, the Yukon became one of the most famous places on earth for trophy hunters. The Yukon wolf was about to meet a new competitor that had no interest in sharing wildlife.

6

A Bounty of Fur

Clarence Lagoon - March 1928

I t is bitterly cold but today he must hunt. He shot seven caribou in the summer and dried the long strips of meat on the great weathered logs that cover the Arctic beach in front of his driftwood home. The meat is nearly gone. He should have killed ten more this winter, but he has seen none. He is worried and senses his wife's quiet distress. His children are still asleep in the home he fashioned from the bleached logs, salvaged planks, and timbers he combed from the beaches. He wakes his wife who lies beside him. She emerges silently from a jumble of caribou skins and heavy wool blankets. She dresses and lights the iron cook stove. Soon heat fills their home.

When it is warm he climbs from the bed, pulls on his light caribou shirt, and slips the anorak over his head. The anorak is old and most of the hairs are broken and worn. He rubs his hands over his waist. He must soon replace it with a new one. Perhaps today he will be lucky and kill caribou. He pulls his leather pants over long woolen underwear, and slips on wool socks and sealskin mukluks.

The white men call this place Clarence Lagoon. It is beside Alaska, but the invisible boundary that passes through Demarcation Point has never made a difference to him. His native Inuit tongue is Uummarmiutun, but he knows English also because of the many whalers who lived on Herschel Island only twenty miles away. The whalers are gone but there is still a store and police post there. A few Inuvialuit families have built homes from the jumble of driftwood that floated from the mouth of the Mackenzie River, eventually ending up on the barren Yukon coast. They are here because the lagoon fills with thousands of spawning whitefish and char trout in summer, and there is always plenty of driftwood for building and heating their homes. There are seals on the shore ice, thousands of Porcupine caribou have their calves and summer on the coastal plain, and there are berries to collect in the mountains only a few miles to the south. It is a summer paradise. In winter it can be a place of starvation.

Only the best trappers and hunters live along the Yukon coastal plain. It is always windy here and ocean storms come without warning, making travel dangerous. Storms and high winds can send huge waves over the beaches soaking homes a hundred meters inland. The mountains nearly touch the ocean here, and this is what makes the weather so unpredictable and severe. He has been caught in storms out along on the coast, escaping into the temporary driftwood shelters his people have built for just such emergencies.

He has trapped for fox since November but he has not caught a single animal. The dog sickness has killed them off. He travels in all directions from the Lagoon but there is no fox, no wolverine – and no caribou. His dogs are always hungry. Now they are barking outside as the daylight approaches, reminding him that he is failing as a hunter. The supply of dried fish he netted last summer is getting dangerously low. He must kill something today for his hungry dogs and for his family.

His long sled creaks and groans as it bumps and slides over the windblown snow. It is difficult to see tracks on the hard-packed surface, but his eyes have been trained since he was a young boy to see subtle change in snow patterns and texture showing where something living has passed – a single toe print of a fox, a small crack in a drift where a caribou foot has broken through, or a wolf foot pad.

His dogs suddenly stop and sniff at the ground. His eyes follow the line of prints breaking the irregular wind patterns in the snow far into the distance. He walks to the tracks and kneels down to examine the details closely. He cannot easily distinguish prints, which means the pack is large. He pushes his fingers in the track and can feel the harder edge of the tracks indicating they are heading south into the mountains. As he walks back to the sled he hears the faint call of a raven somewhere in the far off hills. He pulls off the wolverine-trimmed parka hood and listens carefully. He hears it again and marks the place on the horizon. Ravens can mean wolf kill or it could mean nothing. He swings the dogs onto the wolf trail and follows it across the coastal plain toward the mountains on the horizon.

The gray wolf on the ridge disappears somewhere ahead in the creek as the sled slips noisily along the smooth, turquoise-blue ice. It has spotted him, but he cannot avoid being seen here. Three ravens glide along the windless ridge calling excitedly. Wolves and ravens mean caribou are here. He is becoming excited and checks the snow along the creek for caribou tracks but there is nothing. He pulls his 30:30 Winchester rifle from the canvas scabbard strapped to the sled, levers a shell into the chamber and slips the hammer to half cock. The komatik sled bumps noisily along the ice as he rounds a corner of the creek. He catches a movement from the corner of his eye and spots the wolves walking high along the slope to his right. He counts six. Then a few seconds later another five appear behind them. They are 600 meters away – too far for a shot. The wolves are light – almost white, and he wishes they were closer. The white ones are the most valuable for parka trim, and he could trade two pelts for a month's supply of provisions at the Herschel Island store. He watches the wolves and their expensive ruffs disappear over the ridge. The sound of excited ravens returns his interest back to the creek ahead.

Three cow caribou carcasses are scattered through the low shrubs along the creek. They are completely stripped of meat, the hides shredded and useless. The leg bones have been cracked and the marrow is gone. There are two heads worth salvaging. He cuts them off with a small axe and puts them under the canvas covering the sled. The dogs are excited by the smell. They are howling and barking, hungry and anxious for a fresh meat meal. A fight breaks out, and he sprints for the two offenders and pummels them both with hard blows, breaking them up.

He moves the team up the creek looking for caribou to hunt. This time of year they will be coming from where the sun rises. And they will be traveling the snow free mountain ridges where travel is easiest. But no one in Clarence Lagoon has seen caribou in these mountains since summer. He does not remember a winter in his thirty-five years when the caribou did not finally come. But there are caribou here now. And more must be coming – many more.

His sled winds through the shallow snow up the narrow valley. The creek ice soon disappears, and he traverses across the face of mountain slopes holding the komatik on the uphill runner to keep it from tipping. The snow near the ridge has been blown away by winter winds. He stops the dogs before the runners grind into the black rock and gravel. He pulls out his axe and drives a pin into the frozen ground to secure the sled. He crouches down and walks carefully ahead, cradling his loaded rifle in his arms. As he approaches the ridgeline, the broad valley of the Malcolm River slowly appears below. He stops and scans the rolling tundra for tracks and animal movement. After a few minutes he makes out the dark shapes moving against the shimmering snow far off in the middle of the valley. From their smooth loping cadence, their long shape and low profile he knows immediately they are wolves. They are far away, and he knows he could not approach them without being seen. They are following a wide caribou trail that has come from the Firth River to the east. He sits on the hard gravel and pulls out the small spotting glass from his jacket, resting his elbows on his knees to stabilize the instrument. He counts fifteen wolves – seven blacks and eight grays. He scans the entire valley but there are no caribou in sight.

He carefully considers the opportunity. The sun is high now, and he could be in shooting range in two or three hours. He checks the horizon for weather and confirms the wind direction. It is cloudless; the wind is blowing from the south – from the wolves toward him. There is just enough time if everything goes smoothly. He turns to ready his team for the chase.

Suddenly he hears a howl somewhere close behind. He swings his spotting glass down into the lower river valley and sees another pack. He counts nine wolves resting a few hundred meters from a fresh caribou kill a kilometer below him near the edge of the Malcolm River. He stuffs the scope under the canvas sled cover, then moves his team down behind the long ridge where the wolves cannot see them. He nudges the sled forward slowly, careful to keep the dogs from barking or yelping. A light wind is blowing up the ridge from the wolves - perfect conditions for a hunt. He keeps below the skyline and out of view of the wolves. Halfway down the ridge he stops the team. He opens the canvas covers of the komatik and pulls out a small white canvas sheet. He moves across the gravel on his hands and knees, and peers over the ridge toward the wolves. The pack is 500 meters below. He can see three wolves sleeping on the open tundra just above the kill and another is asleep on his side of the river. The rest of the wolves have moved uphill.

He opens the sheet and pulls his head through the hole cut in the centre, and begins his slow stalk downhill. It takes him nearly an hour to work his way down through the shallow snow to a band of low bushes along the river. He moves a few meters and stops each time, careful not to attract the attention of the wolves. As he nears the bottom of the valley he crawls over a small hill that houses the wolf den that he has passed by countless times on his journeys into these mountains. The den has been freshly dug out. The wolves in front of him are preparing to have pups here. It is a good sign that caribou will calve among these hills and there will be a good summer of hunting. He is now two hundred meters from the nearest wolf and partly hidden behind a large boulder near the river. He is close enough for a shot. As he watches, two black wolves emerge from behind a low hill and walk to the caribou carcass near the river. They begin tugging off strips of flesh. He raises his rifle and sights in on the closest one.

The faint sounds of his dogs barking breaks the Arctic silence. The two wolves stop feeding and look high to the ridge behind him. The sleeping one slowly stands and cocks its head to find where the barking is coming from. His years of hunting experience take over. He shifts into high but controlled speed. The two wolves turn slowly broadside offering a brief but perfect pair of targets. The wolves do not know the difference between barking dogs and their own kind, so he uses the moment to take advantage of their curiosity. He rests the 30:30 rifle barrel on the side of the boulder and finds the first wolf in the v-notch of his open sights. He holds steady on the wolf with a full bead above the notch of the rear sight and gently squeezes the trigger. The sharp crack of the rifle echoes around the mountain valley. The bullet hits the wolf with a dull smack. It crumbles onto its chest. He pulls the lever ejecting the spent shell, chambers a new round, finds the other one looking straight at him, and fires again. The bullet hits the wolf through the lower shoulder as it is turning to run away. It spins, stumbles and drops motionless onto the blue ice.

He swings the barrel widely knowing the third wolf will be running. It is a much more difficult shot. He holds his bare finger lightly on the trigger, and waits. He knows the wolf will eventually stop and look back – but when, how far away? At 400 meters it stops on the tundra and offers him one shot. He holds the sights a meter above the top of the wolf's back and half a meter to the left to adjust for the south wind blowing. He fires. The wolf instantly spins backwards and crumples onto the hard snow. The hunter stands up and looks over the boulder for the others. Three wolves are far away running along the shimmering pan of river ice. Three more are working their way up the ridge to his left, and well out of range.

He climbs quickly back to the top of the ridge where he finds his dogs sleeping. They wake and begin their wild chorus as he nears the team. He unpins the sled, and moves the team carefully down the slope onto the river, working his way through the boulders and slick ice to the closest wolf. He pulls a long skinning knife from his waist and opens each wolf's belly, careful not to cut into the distended stomachs filled with steamy caribou meat. He slices through the diaphragm and stuffs his hand high on the rubbery esophagus. With a single cut he pulls out the steaming entrails then packs each cavity with snow to cool the carcasses down. This will keep their valuable hair from slipping off the hide. He carries the wolves to the komatik and lays them down so they do not touch. He carries piles of snow in his hands filling the komatik, and leaves the canvas cover open so the carcasses can cool.

He moves his team across the river to the third wolf. This is an adult female and it's still alive, her spinal chord badly shattered by the bullet. It swings its head up toward the shining rifle barrel, but it is unable to move its limbs. The fourth bullet enters the skull behind the ear and takes her life instantly. The hunter repeats the quick gutting and snow packing. He lifts the last wolf into the sled, rubs his hands in the dry snow for a quick cleaning, pulls his large mitts on, and steps onto the back of the sled

The load is too heavy for the dogs to retrace their route back up the long ridge toward home. He will follow the Malcolm River out onto the coastal plain. It is longer this way but no slower than trying to move over the mountains. There is a crescent moon rising in the east, which will help him find his way across the darkening tundra. By the time he reaches the last ridge the sun has set, but there are still hours of twilight to travel. He is about to turn the dogs off the river ice when he catches movement to his right.

A large bull caribou is running at full speed towards him. Four wolves are about two hundred meters behind it. The bull's tongue is hanging from its mouth, and he can see it is nearing exhaustion. The caribou heads for the wind-blown ridge where it tries to outdistance the wolves on an uphill race. In the fading light the caribou and wolves have not yet seen him and his team.

He only has a few seconds. He pulls the rifle from the scabbard and raises the stock to his shoulder. There is no time to find a shooting rest. He aims for the left side the bull but it is quartering away now leaving little target area. The caribou makes the base of the ridge and scrambles up the slope kicking snow and gravel. It is running for its life. The wolves are now only a few meters behind the caribou when the report of the rifle pierces the silence. His shot is low and it misses the caribou. The wolves twist and turn to see the cause of the great noise. They instantly abort their hunt, and head down the ridge toward the coastal plain and the safety of the grey darkness. The wolves are moving away from him as he lays his rifle along the back of the komatik, and fires two rounds at the closest one. As he pulls the trigger he can feel the first bullet will be too high. He drops his next shot slightly and brings the trailing wolf down. The others run further onto the darkening plain. In a few minutes they are out of sight.

He stands with his arms akimbo for some time watching the wolves disappear. He has learned much from them, and he silently thanks the wolf spirit for a good day of hunting.

He moves to his sled, clicks his tongue at the dogs, and the team pulls the heavy sled into motion. He processes and loads the last wolf into the komatik. He knows he will be home when the moon settles behind Herschel Island. Tomorrow he will travel to the store there and buy badly needed provisions for his family. He is a hunter again. He pulls his parka hood up and his team picks up speed.

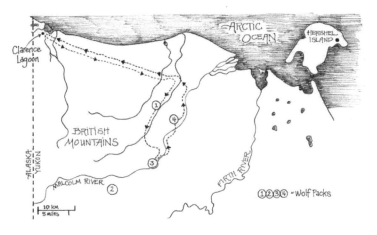

based this narrative on a letter written by Royal Canadian Mounted Police constable Kemp who was stationed at Herschel Island in the northern Yukon in 1928. Kemp wrote that wolves had killed quite a few caribou in the mountains south of Herschel Island. Local Inuvialuit hunters had not been able to kill any caribou all winter, and the fur catch was very poor. Kemp wrote, "A native from Clarence Lagoon informs me that on a hunt he made for caribou he saw only one such animal alive, but came across several carcasses killed by wolves. On the same trip he saw no fewer than 40 wolves." Kemp ends the letter recommending a bounty on Yukon wolves. This letter underscores a significant shift in attitude about wolves. In the first two decades of the 1900s, wolves transformed from a largely insignificant carnivore to a major competitor and threat to the livelihood of both native and non-native people. Wolf behavior did not change, but human attitudes certainly did.

Before the 1900s Yukon explorers and naturalist hardly mentioned wolves. Robert Campbell does not write about wolves in his exploration of the upper Liard River drainage for the Hudson's Bay Company during the 1840s. Frederick Schwatka's book *Along Alaska's Great River* does not mention wolves on his 2,000-mile journey down the Yukon River in the late 1800s, nor does Tappan Adney's The *Klondike Stampede*. W.H. Osgood carried out the first biological survey of the Yukon River region in 1900. He makes one comment about wolves, "The country along the Yukon is not well suited for wolves and they are seldom seen there." In 1911, Charles Sheldon wrote this summary about wolves in *The Wilderness of the Upper Yukon*:

"Wolves exist throughout the Territory, but are quite local in their haunts. The black phase of color is common. They tend to keep pretty close to caribou in localities where caribou are common. Their habits are similar to those of timber wolves elsewhere."

The wolf was of little consequence or interest to these early historians, hunters, and naturalists. By 1910, most of the Klondike gold seekers had given up on their dreams of striking it rich. Many that stayed turned to trapping to make their living. The proliferation of non-native trappers through the territory soon depleted fur in many areas, especially around Dawson City. In 1910 Francis Congdon, former Commissioner of the Yukon, wrote this in *Fur Bearing Animals and How to Prevent their Extinction*:

"One difference between hunting by trappers and by Indians is that, while the Indian always leaves a stock of all fur bearing animals in a district to continue the species, the white man does not."

Congdon was also prophetic in his view of the future of the Yukon fur industry. He felt the greatest dangers were poisons, over-harvesting, and an increase in the number of wolves. Many Yukoners shared his concern about wolves. Trappers disliked wolves because they raided their traps and stole foxes and marten – both highly valued fur at the time. As fur harvest declined the trapper's dislike of wolves naturally increased.

Yukon hunters soon joined in the rally against the wolf. They complained wolves were the cause of moose and caribou declines around Dawson. Undoubtedly, overharvest by people was an important cause. Moose and caribou were staple foods of native people of the central Yukon, and for the early prospectors and explorers living along the upper Yukon River. Gold miners at Fortymile killed 300 caribou in a single winter during the 1890s. Although this might seem high, hunting was probably sustainable because there were relatively few people living off the land at the time.

The invasion by gold seekers in 1897 vastly increased the number of hungry mouths in the territory, and caused an enormous drain on wildlife in the central Yukon that would last for many decades. Moose and caribou were still abundant when the first gold seekers made their way down the Yukon River. Expecting an endless supply of wild game, these vanguard prospectors carried barely enough supplies to make it through that first winter, relying instead on the bounty of the land. But the following year, the fear of starvation sent many gold seekers out of the Yukon before the snow flew. The thousands that stayed in Dawson City needed food – and they looked to the wilderness refrigerator for it. In 1897, over 150 moose were reported shot around Dawson, but the number was probably much higher in the region.

Market hunters saw the chance to make easy money. Commercial hunters went far and wide to kill moose and caribou, rapidly depleting the game in the Pelly, Stewart, and MacMillan Rivers. A single party of native hunters reportedly killed eighty moose and sixty-five caribou in one winter alone. The near eradication of moose in the central Yukon was rapid. In 1900, W.H. Osgood spent three months along the river and never saw a moose. Hunting soon shifted to caribou. In 1904, market hunters killed 1,500 caribou to feed 9,000 residents of Dawson City.

Around this time a new and sophisticated kind of hunter arrived to add to the pressure on dwindling wildlife populations and begin the persecution of wolves. Wealthy sport hunters from around the world flocked to the Yukon on the heels the gold prospectors attracted by stories of world-record moose and caribou. Sharing a charismatic hunting ethic that was being championed by Teddy Roosevelt, they sought new wilderness places to hunt. And virtually anyone could reach the Yukon in a matter of weeks traveling in comfort by steamship, paddlewheeler or train. Waiting for these eager hunters were the largest moose in the world, great herds of caribou, the fabled white Dall's sheep, and a growing number of would-be big game outfitters.

The sport hunters soon added to the hunting pressures on game populations already taxed by market and subsistence hunting. Gold discoveries in the Chisana and Kluane areas in the early 1900s opened new hunting areas for the legendary Dall's sheep, one of the most sought after big game trophies at the time. Yukoners realized the financial bonanza guiding sport hunters represented, and outfitters sprung up through the territory between 1910 and 1920. Many successful trophy hunters returned home and wrote best-selling books about their Yukon hunting experiences, most notably *Recent Hunting Trips in North America* (1907) by F.C. Selous and *The Wilderness of the Upper Yukon* (1911) by Charles Sheldon. The books became hugely popular with North America hunters and the Yukon soon rivaled the fabled hunting grounds of Africa.

The territorial government quickly recognized the value of trophy hunting to the new economy. In 1908, game laws included a fee of one hundred dollars for a non-resident hunter – a huge amount of money back then. As the hunting economy flourished the laws slowly became more restrictive. Hunting guides required a government license by 1920. Competition for the limited licenses became fierce, and the territorial government banned native people from owning concessions. Johnny Johns, a world famous native hunting guide, gave up his status in order to keep his outfitting area.

By the early 1920s wildlife numbers were in sharp decline. Commercial guides, fox farmers, trappers, subsistence hunters, market hunters, prospectors, and native people all pointed fingers at each other as the cause. Native hunters were accused of being unethical, and they were criticized for poor shooting skills and indiscriminate wounding loss. They were also accused of selling trophies of animals that were supposedly killed for subsistence. Prospectors accused trappers of cleaning out large areas of moose to feed their teams of sled dogs. Market hunters were blamed for the low moose and caribou numbers. Fox farming, one of the biggest Yukon industries in the 1920s was blamed for illegally killing moose and caribou. But, as is human nature, no one was willing to take responsibility. As big game dwindled through the territory, the wolf soon became the scapegoat that everyone could easily agree on.

By the 1920s, trappers were licensed to poison wolves and coyotes with strychnine baits. Native people strongly opposed this practice arguing poison would kill many other valued fur species. The opposition against poison would grow through the 1920s, but the practice remained widespread. In 1927, F. Laderoute, a trapper, wrote a letter of complaint to territorial officials that contains the longest sentence I know:

"I understand Mr. William Gooley got a permit by his sweet tongue from the police to set out poison at three creeks on left limit of Yukon and no limit to the lengths of time he has no date mentioned and as I am working on island on opposite Independent Creek and I have valuable sheep dogs that follow me I object to him holding a permit for Independent Creek, and fancy that the other two creeks are enough for him to use poison on and if it was right looked into there would not be any poison used on any of these Creeks as it's a fur country and we all know that all other furs will take the bate and hide under old flood and they are never found and ask you to notify him for my sake and other for him not to have to use poison and you will oblige and I will ever pray."

Financial incentives were also introduced to increase the number of wolves trapped. From 1923 to 1929 the trapper who killed the most wolves was awarded $500, the second highest was awarded $300, and the third $200 – as much money as they might make all year on their traplines. The incentive ended when some trappers were inevitably discovered pooling their wolves to share in the lucrative payouts.

By the late 1920s big game populations were hitting rock bottom, so public pressure was turned up on wolves. The Yukon Commissioner wrote letters to the federal government chronicling the increase of the 'pests' all over the territory. Police reported large numbers of wolves in various areas. A poison application was received from a Stewart River resident because they were "...losing their moose mighty fast out there because of wolves." Wolves were especially abundant in the Pelly River area where two men took thirty-seven wolves in 1928, likely with the aid of poison. On the distant Yukon Arctic coast there were complaints of abundant wolves and no caribou. The Commissioner believed that a wolf bounty would be a popular move with Yukoners. British Columbia and Alaska were also preparing to introduce bounties in response to public concern about dwindling wildlife. So the time was ripe for a Yukon bounty.

In some ways, the introduction of a wolf bounty was inevitable. By 1928, fur accounted for six hundred thousand dollars in the Yukon revenues matching the gold output that year. Protecting the fur industry had become as important as protecting gold dust and big game outfitters. In July 1929, the Yukon Territorial Council proclaimed a thirty-dollar bounty on wolves and a fifteen-dollar bounty on coyotes. They set aside twenty-five thousand dollars in the budget to cover expected payouts. The territorial agents thought bounties would increase the take of wolves and coyotes, but they were in for a surprise. Only forty-three wolves and twenty-four coyotes were submitted for bounty. The payout was just over $2,000 – less than 10 percent of the allotted budget.

The low public response to the bounties was purely bureaucratic. The reporting process was quite onerous for anyone claiming a wolf or coyote. The applicant was required to present a properly cleaned hide with no flesh or fat attached. The ear was marked with a punch to ensure no duplicate payment was made. Wolf warrants required more details: who killed the wolf and where, the date, the sex, and whether the applicant was 'Indian, half-breed, Eskimo or white'. To many Yukoners – and the rather disgruntled agents – the process was a waste of time for the small amount of money paid. To top it off, providing such mundane information was against the independent code of Yukoners who – to this day – like to view themselves as more sensible than 'outsiders'. The low bounty take in 1929 was due to the lack of public trust in the bounty reporting system, not because there were fewer wolves and coyotes killed.

Did poison baits and bounties help reduce wolf predation on big game in the 1920s? It seems not. There were no reports of game populations increasing anywhere in the Yukon during the decade. This is no surprise because the number of wolves killed each year was far too small to have caused a noticeable decline in wolves. The wolf population in the 1920s was probably similar to what it is now – about 5,000 animals. The annual harvest through the 1920s never exceeded a couple of hundred wolves – less than 3 percent of the population – too low to have made any difference in their overall numbers. Wolves are highly productive and can sustain annual losses of over 30 percent before the population sees a noticeable drop the next year. On the other hand, the wolverine harvest was in the order of 10-15 percent of the population using the present-day estimate of 4,000 Yukon wolverines. For the relatively unproductive wolverine, this loss was too much, causing a decline in their numbers in some regions.

In response to growing public concern, poison was finally outlawed in the Yukon in 1931, but there was still plenty of cheap strychnine in the territory and the law could not be enforced anyway. Many trappers continued to use poisons on their lines for years. Officials turned a blind-eye to what they saw was an unpopular and unnecessary ban. In 1933, the bounty was repealed after trappers continued to show little interest. The reported export of wolf pelts between 1931 and 1933 averaged only twenty-five then it increased dramatically, averaging 473 animals from 1934 to 1939, the highest harvest ever recorded in the Yukon.

Then came the Second World War and the threat of a Japanese attack on the United States, which brought thousands of U.S. military personnel north to build a road connecting Alaska with the rest of the continent. In less than a year, the army pushed a rough road through the Yukon. The instant influx of so many soldiers caught the sleepy Yukon by surprise. For decades Yukoners had been left to their own devices, but the construction of the Alaska Highway suddenly changed everything.

Faced with the threat of thousands of new American mouths to feed, the Territorial Council chose naiveté and indecision in place of good governance. In 1942, against the advice of the Government of Canada, The Territorial Council amended the Yukon Game Ordinance to sell all U.S. personnel a resident hunting license for one dollar. No doubt the offer was partly in support of the war effort, but the opportunity to collect easy money from the new hunters also played into the decision. On the other hand, Alaska implemented harvest restrictions and established game sanctuaries in advance of the road construction. There were no limits on hunting activities of crews in the Yukon, with the exception of a new game sanctuary to protect the world famous Dall's sheep population in the Kluane area. The Territorial Council's solution was to turn a blind-eye to the juggernaut of men, machines and military rifles rolling through the southern Yukon.

Moose, caribou, mountain goat, and Dall's sheep became the staple meat of road construction crews. Many areas along the Alaska Highway route were cleaned out of game as the road building progressed. Harvest was never monitored so it will never be known how many animals were killed to feed soldiers while they were on Yukon soil. By the end of the war the result was a great loss of game in the southern Yukon. The issuing of resident licenses to U.S. soldiers embittered many Yukoners for years to come. The wolf bounty was reinstated in 1949 as a token gesture to address the slaughter. In 1949 George Black, Yukon Member of Parliament, wrote this scathing introduction to J.E. Gibbens the newly appointed Commissioner of the Yukon:

"During the last American invasion of the southern Yukon the invaders practically exterminated the game, fish, animals and birds. Unless checked and watched it will be repeated.

Your predecessor (Jeckell) treated them as residents. They fished and killed and left their victims to rot."

The legacy of Yukon game mismanagement during the 1940s did not go unnoticed. In 1949, a highly critical article in the popular magazine *Look* exposed the nearly non-existent enforcement of Yukon game laws. At the same time the fledgling Yukon Fish and Game Association became a political force, promoting the introduction of elk, bison and deer to the Yukon to replace depleted wild game and to increase hunting opportunities for resident hunters. Yukon outfitters said moose and caribou numbers were declining quickly and the wolf was the main cause. The storm was gathering for more wolf control. In the mid 1940s, many game associations in western Canada lobbied for the outright destruction of wolves, claiming the carnivores were the cause of major declines in big game in the provinces. Sentiment against the Yukon wolf was also growing among politicians, fueled by the powerful lobbying of the Yukon Fish and Game Association. Simply put, wolves were taking away hunting opportunities for residents and outfitters. George Black, Yukon Member of Parliament, wrote Commissioner Gibbens warning of the high losses of big game due to wolves. His letter concludes,

"The use of poison by trustworthy reliable men would go far towards preserving a fast disappearing valuable public asset."

7

Poison from Heaven

Dawson City - 14 April 1954

The morning sun is already high in the eastern sky, but inside the plane it is very cold. It may be spring in the rest of the world, but in Dawson City winter has not yet loosened its icy tendrils. The pistons of the Cessna 180 are pounding hard as the plane taxis to the end of the gravel strip. The pilot checks his instruments for takeoff. The engine slowly roars to life as the small plane rolls down the runway, lumbering into the air. The game warden is strapped into a sling seat far in the back recess of the cockpit. The right front seat has been removed for the cargo. There is a mountain of gunnysacks piled waist high from his feet to the front console.

He scrapes the frost from the back window as the plane levels a few thousand feet above the Klondike River and gains air speed. To the south, he sees the famous Klondike gold fields spreading across the horizon – Discovery Creek, Indian River, Bonanza Creek, Bear Creek – first tilled by the thousands of Klondike gold-seekers with nothing but muscle and shovel. In recent times, the huge gold dredges clawed their way down the same creeks turning the valleys upside down as they dug for legendary Klondike gold.

The plane passes over hundreds of acres of snow covered gravel mounds, then slowly swings to the north, passing over the crippled hulk of Bear Creek No. 4 dredge. Far away are the headwaters of the North Klondike River – the first drop area. The warden watches for signs of life on the river below, but only sees the odd moose tracks and a trail of a single wolf before the plane climbs out of the valley. Soon the high mountain glacier comes into view.

As they near the snow-covered mountains the plane is suddenly buffeted by strong winds. He feels the familiar yawing of the fuselage as the first mountain wave catches the wings, slamming the plane downward and sideways into a heavy shudder. He shuffles forward on his low seat so his head does not bang against the window. The ground winds are tearing at the surface snow on the knife-edge ridges forming a sparkling veil across the mountain slope. The Cessna makes a tight turn upwind following the contours of the steep mountain. The warden kneels forward preparing himself for his move. He looks at the pilot who silently nods then he carefully unlatches the right door. He will have to be quick in these dangerous winds. He checks the string tying the paper bags to the bait sack. He shakes each bag feeling the frozen strychnine pellets roll loosely inside.

The pilot feathers back the power and the plane drops down over the glacier. The warden grabs the top of the gunnysack with his left hand and pushes the door open with his right forearm. A shock of frozen air instantly fills the cockpit. He snatches the sack, heaving it out of the plane in one fluid motion. The bag sails out and disappears. He pulls the door shut and pushes his face to the window just as the bait sack hits the ground. The two paper bags silently explode onto the glacier, casting the pellets everywhere. He crouches by the window as the Cessna 180 circles above the drop site. The bait sack is lying on its side unbroken. The strychnine pellets are scattered everywhere – a perfect drop.

The plane banks and levels off as they cross the divide into the upper Blackstone River watershed. There are no signs of life in the high mountain plateau except for a wolf trail that is quickly blowing in with snow. The warden pulls a yellow pencil from his parka pocket. He takes the folded map from the floor and scribbles the location, 64° 25'N and 138° 15'W. Leaning forward, he points to the next drop site on the map – Chapman Lake. The pilot checks the map and nods.

The second drop also goes perfectly. The bait sack holds and the strychnine pellets explode from the paper bags just as planned. The Cessna climbs once more then heads down the Blackstone River. Before he climbs back to his seat he nudges the pilot's shoulder and holds his thumb up.

Signs of life begin to appear along the river valley below. Soon they are flying over heavy caribou trails and feeding craters scattered through the thin spruce forest below. But there are no caribou in sight; only the tracks of willow ptarmigan, snowshoe hare, moose, wolf, and fox winding through the shrubby flats bordering the river. He was expecting to see big game, but so far he has seen none.

Soon the Cessna is circling over the drop area on the Blackstone River. This time the drop goes badly. A paper bag is torn away from the sack before it hits the ground. It spirals down to the river ice where the wind blows it into the willows. The second paper bag containing pellets has not opened. It is flapping in the wind against the bait sack. The plane is equipped with skis but they can't land on the narrow river, so they head east for the Hart River following heavy caribou trails to the river mouth. They successfully drop bait at the mouth of Lomon Creek. He checks his map – four drops so far; six more to go before heading back to Dawson City.

He hears a shout and looks up from his map. The pilot points to the right side of the plane and yells, "Wolves ahead! On your side." The plane dips hard to the right and he glimpses three wolves running fast over the hard snow on the river. The pilot slams the throttle forward, banks the plane clockwise and returns over the wolves.

"That's a wide trail, there must be more than three", the warden shouts. But the heavy Cessna has too much fuel and cargo onboard to safely circle here. The wolves slow down after some minutes and begin walking, apparently oblivious of the plane circling above. The warden checks his map and sees Worm Lake is not far upriver. He leans forward and lifts the map to the pilot and silently points to the lake. A few minutes later they drop bait on the icy lake surface. The warden records the location at $64°$ 36'N and $136°$ 16'W.

As they fly south, they pass out of the Peel River watershed and into the Stewart River basin. The warden pulls a bag lunch from a small pack and pours two cups of steaming coffee from a thermos. He passes a cup to the pilot. Twenty minutes later they drop bait on a narrow section of McQuesten Lake. They fly to Reid Lakes, passing over the Dawson Road. Reid Lakes always has wolf sign, but today there are no tracks breaking the soft blanket of snow covering the lake. They continue northwest along the Dawson Road, dropping the rest of the baits before the Cessna 180 touches back down in Dawson.

The warden walks to his truck, glad to have his legs firmly on the ground. He is feeling a discomforting tinge of airsickness but feels better after hauling more gunnysacks to the plane while the pilot refuels. He checks his watch. The sun will not set until 10:00 tonight – eight hours from now. He can finish his job so long as the weather holds. The plane is airborne once again, this time heading west to the Sixtymile River country where they drop four baits. Caribou craters and winter trails fill the spruce forest below. He is constantly on the lookout for game, but sees only a few straggling caribou headed north to summer range.

The sun is still high in the sky when the plane touches back down in Dawson City. The Cessna 180 rolls off the gravel runway onto the apron. The pilot switches off the key and the engine sputters to a halt. The warden sits up and does a careful check of the cockpit floor to make sure no poison bags or loose pellets have accidentally fallen from the sacks. He stuffs his map in the briefcase and pulls off his sunglasses. As he rubs his tired eyes he is thinking how much country they flew and how little wolf sign they have seen.

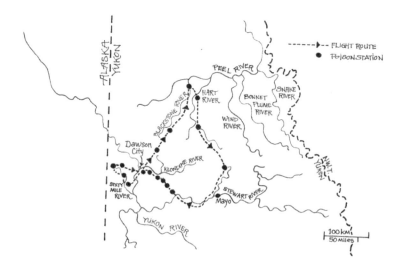

based this narrative on details contained in a field report filed by the Dawson City game warden in 1954. In addition to the fifteen aerial baits, he placed two others near Dawson City by truck. There was no money to patrol the airdrops, but he did check the road sites regularly. One near the airport produced no wolf kills, but unknown animals or birds took several poison pellets. One poisoned red fox was found which some Dawson City residents viewed with disapproving eyes. The other bait was placed at a moose carcass that died near Discovery Pup. A week later eight pellets disappeared, then a week later a young female wolf was found poisoned at the site. A few days later a large male wolf was found about 500 meters from the bait. The warden noted:

"It is impossible to tell how many kills were made at this set unless a thorough inspection of the area was made, as it can be readily understood that all kills would not be found in timbered country when an animal can travel at least a third of a mile after taking poison."

Poison flights were commonplace during the 1950s when wolf control was the main field activity carried out by the newly formed Game Department. There were no biologists studying wildlife populations back then, but there was strong public sentiment that game was low and still dropping. Wolf predation was blamed and reports of packs of 40-50 wolves near Pelly Crossing and Whitehorse were all the evidence needed.

Them Kjar (pronounced 'tem care') led the poison campaign. He was hired in 1949 as the first director of the Yukon Game and Publicity Department. His appointment was fast tracked following the *Look* magazine article that strongly criticized the territory for its dismal lack of game regulations. Desperate to save political face and protect hunting businesses, the Territorial Council hired Kjar out of Alberta where he had gained considerable experience poisoning wolves and coyotes in the ranchlands.

Poisoning began immediately. Kjar introduced cyanide guns or 'coyote-getters' first. Cyanide guns fire poison from a blank cartridge into an animal's mouth when it tugs on a trigger baited with meat or a scented lure. The cyanide experiment was short-lived because the Yukon Territory was simply too large to deploy and monitor the complicated devices. A simpler and easier way to spread poison was needed. Within a few years Kjar had his full-scale strychnine poison program up and running. In 1954, the Game Branch dropped 1,400 kilograms of bait and 3,500 strychnine pellets from airplane at seventy-two locations. In 1953, the Territorial Council repealed the wolf bounty that had been on the books since 1946, anticipating great results from Kjar's poison program. By 1956 the territorial government, the Yukon Fish and Game Association, big game guides, and the Canadian Wildlife Service were all involved in the poisoning. That year was the peak of the campaign when 2,700 kilograms of bait and 6,500 pellets were dropped at 154 stations around the territory.

Them Kjar knew the ins and outs of strychnine and he was a hands-on director. He personally prepared baits, which must have consumed a large part of his time through the year. His staff was always searching for baits to distribute the poison. They collected, butchered and froze road-killed moose and caribou, and hand prepared thousands of strychnine pellets for the winter campaigns. The knowledge of how to prepare poison pellets became commonplace, even among the least likely staff. When Kjar was away his secretary wrote this exquisite recipe on poison bait preparation in a letter to Maurice Kelly, the predator control supervisor for Alaska.

"A pellet batter is equal parts white flour and corn meal. Mix enough water then make the dough so that it can be handled, not sticky, but moist enough to stick together when rolled. A large handful of dough is rolled out on a table into a long roll an inch in diameter then sliced with a sharp knife into pieces about ¾ of an inch thick. Each piece is then rolled into a small ball and then flattened to form a 'cookie' – 1 to 1 ½ inches in diameter. The strychnine tablets are picked up carefully with tweezers and placed in the centre of the cookie. They are pinched together and the cookie is rolled into a tightly sealed ball and placed in a sieve. The sieve is dipped into a pan containing animal blood (either pork, beef or wild game blood) and whale oil, the proportions of approximately one part whale oil to nine parts blood. When the pellets have dripped for a moment, they are put into a flat pan containing seal meal, and are rolled in the seal meal until completely covered. They are then set in a cold room to freeze. As soon as the pellets are frozen, 30 of them are placed in a paper bag, which is tied to the sack of frozen bait to be dropped on remote lakes, thereby establishing a lethal station. Pellets must be kept frozen so they do not stick to each other when dropped."

This cookbook-style recipe might have impressed Betty Crocker, but the grim truth is strychnine is a most deadly poison, causing dramatic and extremely painful symptoms for any unfortunate beast that might ingest it. Strychnine is an alkaloid derived from the seeds of *Strychnos nux vomica* a small tree of the East Indies. It is one of the bitterest substances known. Its acrid taste is detectable in concentrations as low as one part per million.

The poison action is quick and deadly. Ten minutes after ingesting strychnine, a wolf becomes visibly restless. Its muscles start to twitch and its neck becomes hard. Soon the neck and head muscles begin to spasm uncontrollably. The spasms quickly spread to every muscle until the animal is in a constant state of excruciating convulsion. The slightest noise or touch is enough to trigger a new round of shaking. The spasms intensify until the wolf's backbone is twisting and arching continually. In immense pain for a few hours, it finally dies from asphyxiation caused by paralysis of the nerves that control breathing, or from sheer exhaustion brought on by the steady convulsions. At the moment of death the wolf's body freezes as rigor mortis instantly sets in. In a typical death pose the poisoned wolf is found on its side its limbs extended straight out. Strychnine is a very bad way for any living thing to die.

Despite the widespread aerial campaign, only fifty-four poisoned wolves were recovered in 1956 – a ratio of one wolf killed for every three bait stations, or one wolf for every 120 poison pellets. Follow-up flights were infrequent so more wolves were certainly killed, but how many will never be known. Kjar was resolutely defensive about the low kill results of his campaign. He speculated that undetected wolves moved off the baits and died in the forest never to be accounted for. By June 1956 he became increasingly frustrated by the Territorial Council's complaints about his disappointing results. He wrote his own complaint to W. Gill of the British

Columbia Game Department, who presumably had a more sympathetic ear than Kjar's political bosses:

"Wise men (Territorial Councilors) up to present, have become very skeptical as to results obtained by plane distribution of lethal baits on our wolf populations. I have been only granted a paltry yearly appropriation of two thousand dollars. In many cases I could only find tufts of hair, parts of tail, foot, or the like and I was, by pure luck, only able to discover some of the wolf carcasses buried entirely in the snow. Many wolves with full stomachs travel several miles before collapsing."

Kjar also complained to Alaska's Maurice Kelly writing, "I had to do it all by myself." This was patently untrue, and the statement seems more of an allusion to his paltry budget. But Kjar did have good reason to feel alone and frustrated. He had a tiny staff, a small budget, and unreasonably high expectations to kill lots of wolves. Kelly's response must have galled him. He replied that the Alaska wolf control annual budget was $89,000, enough to pay for six full-time and four part-time staff. Five planes, six boats, and five trucks were dedicated to Alaska wolf control. And unlike Yukon efforts, the Alaskan program reduced wolf numbers broadly through the state.

But Kjar still painted a successful Yukon program despite contrary evidence. Others echoed that wolf poison was working. C.F. Dalziel, a pilot from Watson Lake, wrote to Kjar in 1956 saying he had seen twenty poisoned wolves on baits stations in the Liard River area. He added:

"Whether or not the government feels the money well spent, I do know game, particularly moose, have increased substantially in the areas we have poisoned, both in the Yukon and British Columbia and personally I feel it is a job well done."

Kjar was no biologist. He had no way to compare differences in the game populations where wolves were poisoned to areas where they were not. A mild winter in 1956 could have just as likely been the cause of high moose calf survival that year. But Kjar believed strychnine was paying off. And who could blame him with the intense political scrutiny he was under?

The truth is poison had little effect on wolves or Yukon big game populations. In 1956 the campaign removed only 1 percent of the 5,000 wolves in the territory. Even if ten times as many wolves were poisoned, the program would still not have caused the wolf population to decline in 1957. Our studies in the Yukon more than thirty years later found a sharp increase in moose calf survival happened only after more than 75 percent of the wolves were removed from an area. The strychnine campaign was too broad and diluted to have made any difference to wolf numbers.

The 1950s poison campaign was also unfocused. Baits were often deployed wherever trappers, the Royal Canadian Mounted Police, or big game outfitters reported heavy wolf activity. Information was never verified, and the poison was dropped wherever it seemed best. For example, in February 1957 Jimmie Joe of Aishihik Lake penciled a note on the back of a cancelled check of the Canadian Imperial Bank of Commerce, then mailed it to the Game Branch.

"This is to be given to Mr. Them Kjar. Charles Stevens just got back two weeks ago from trapping he don't do so well on account the wolf been too bad he told me he saw few places wolf kill the moose left the whole moose they don't even touch it he use the meet for the dogs he said he have to build the fire around the dogs so to keep the wolf away every time he go after the squirrel snare he saw the band of wolf himself he think there will be no more moose if wolf keep up that way."

The note closes with a list of lakes that should be poisoned. A few weeks later 270 kilograms of bait and hundreds of strychnine pellets were dropped exactly where Jimmie Joe instructed.

Kjar retired from his position after eight years. On his last day of work on 29 March 1957 he was still obsessed with wolves. He wrote to Frank Butler, Game Commissioner of British Columbia. Butler had asked Kjar to drop poison baits along the Alsek River just inside the British Columbia border. Kjar wrote ten baits were dropped, noting the aircraft crew saw many wolf tracks along the river. No one would ever know how many wolves were poisoned, or if their deaths changed the fate of an Alsek moose.

In June 1957, G.R. Bidlake became the Director of the Game Branch. Bidlake worked under Kjar and learned what not to do. If he was going to succeed in taking more wolves, he needed a better poison campaign. He immediately began amassing lots of bait. Burns Meats in Whitehorse offered to supply him horsemeat at twenty cents a pound; guide Louis Brown of Mayo sold a horse for fifty dollars; slaughtered horses from Fort St. John were delivered to Whitehorse. By early winter Bidlake had begun the next stage of Yukon wolf poisoning.

Bidlake watched Kjar's frustrated attempts to convince the Territorial Council of the merits of the strychnine aerial drops. Bidlake wanted to count dead wolves, not argue that they were dead somewhere under a spruce tree. He cancelled the airdrops and the tedious production of strychnine pellets ended. Instead, his crew followed the Alaskan method. They flew in planes to remote lakes and rivers and froze large pieces of meat laced with strychnine into the ice. Bidlake hoped the large baits would keep wolves nearby until the strychnine began to do its deadly work. Two small trees were frozen into the ice as a courtesy to the passing trappers and to make it easy to find snow-covered carcasses. Tied to each tree was a small sign showing 'Danger-Poison'. The lake bait stations could be revisited to count the number of wolves killed. Bidlake also had the good sense and foresight to hire a well-known biologist to monitor his campaign, and keep as much of the political heat off himself as possible.

Dr. William A. Fuller was the first Yukon biologist. He arrived in 1956 fresh on the heels of a wolf poison program in the Mackenzie River district of the Northwest Territories. Fuller would monitor and compare the success of the Yukon campaign by counting wolf carcasses at ice-bound bait stations in spring. But after three winters, his results were not much better than Kjar's, killing seventy-one wolves at 127 stations.

Fuller conceded the campaign had no effect on wolves; nor did it benefit caribou or moose in any measurable way. He concluded Yukon wolves were far less abundant compared to their Northwest Territories counterparts. He believed the cost of poisoning so few wolves was too much. But Fuller's work provided some information. He found most poisoned wolves were pups or yearlings. Based on these young ages, Fuller speculated the population was about to increase. Oddly enough, he felt the poison program should continue as a way of indexing changes in the wolf population.

The Territorial Council had a quite different view. After nearly a decade of dismal wolf kill results, they cancelled Fuller's program, but poisoning continued. In 1959 Dr. Arthur Pearson, who would go on to become an internationally recognized bear biologist, replaced Fuller. Faced with the political pressure from guide outfitters Pearson reluctantly participated in poisoning, but began to phase it out, knowing it had no effect on game populations. Between 1960 and 1963, the number fell from eighty to thirty poisoned wolves. By the end of the 1960s the public appetite for poison was waning.

Throughout the decades of poisoning, trappers and native people continually criticized the government program because of the many non-target animals killed. Fox, wolverine, and coyotes were regularly poisoned at bait sites. These mammals are mainly scavengers and are highly susceptible to poison. But other mammals and birds were accidentally killed – lots of them.

In April 1985 I saw the grim results of strychnine poisoning, and I was not prepared for what I found. I received a report of illegal poison bait found near Kluane Lake. I flew to the place in a helicopter. We were hovering over a stand of high shrubs when the wash of the helicopter blades blew up a cloud of tiny feathers. It looked as if someone had blown apart a dozen pillows. As we slowly circled, dead animals began to appear below. We landed on the lakeshore and I walked into the high shrubs. There was a sow grizzly bear crumpled in the trees, two wolves, ten ravens, and six magpies. There were hundreds of dead chickadees everywhere I looked – on the ground and in the willow branches, their tiny white feathers scattered like a dusting of fresh snow. No one was ever charged with the poison, but locals pointed to a well-known outfitter in the area who had lost horses that year to wolves.

The interest in controlling wolves during the 1950s and 1960s was a result of a real belief they were solely responsible for the low game numbers through the Yukon. There was also a real emotional fear that perpetuated the negative view of the wolf during these decades. Wolves killed livestock and pets, and even threatened people. In a short story *Encounter with Wolves*, Donna Clayson remembered as a 12-year-old how people in the village of Haines Junction were frightened by a wolf pack that moved into the community one winter. She describes meeting the wolf pack on her way to school one morning, and comes away wondering how dangerous and unpredictable the wolf really was:

"Even in the cold, my hands were sweating and the hair on the back of my neck felt like it was standing on end. I slowly, but steadily moved toward the further ditch, pointing my weapon in the direction of the threat.

The pack, standing with their heads lower than their massive shoulders, watched as I passed to safety. The last 100 yards seemed forever. I slowly turned my gaze toward the school building, away from the intense staring of those magnificent animals.

Inside the school cloakroom, I took off my coat and mukluks and removed the bullet from the chamber of my gun, then slipped the clip (high caliber 30-06) into my lunch bag. As I leaned my rifle against the wall beside the others, a sense of relief and respect overwhelmed me."

Poison gradually declined until 1972 when strychnine use was greatly restricted in the Yukon. Public attitudes about wolves were slowly shifting in North America in the 1970s.

The environmental movement was just emerging and conservation of large carnivores became the flagship issue. Public sentiment against indiscriminate poisoning grew, especially in urban areas where wolves had disappeared long ago. At the same time, a new tool was developing that made it possible to understand the biology of elusive wild animals. Prototype radiocollars were placed on wild wolves allowing biologist to follow their movements. A new understanding about the ecology of wild wolves began to emerge in the late 1970s, especially in Alaska and Minnesota where the first radiotelemetry studies happened. With the new information about wolf biology, biologists could now design studies that measured the real effects of wolf predation on big game.

A new ethic began to emerge in wolf management – if an agency is planning to kill wolves to increase game then the program should be designed as an experiment with predicted outcomes. Bill Gasaway led the first such experiment. His monograph *Interrelationships of wolves, prey, and man* in interior Alaska was published in 1983, the same time I was hired as the Yukon wolf biologist. Bill became my mentor and he gave me advice on how to design experimental approaches for studying the effects of wolves on big game. So, armed with radiocollars I worked with a team of biologists on the first field studies of Yukon wolves in the last mountain wilderness in North America. The next section of the book describes some of the important and surprising things we learned about wolves and their relations with prey and other carnivores. It also describes the evolution of my understanding of the fallacy of aerial wolf control in elevating Yukon woodland caribou and moose populations.

Part 2 Understanding

Cordillera

Imagine a place in North America that has hardly changed in thousands of years – a half million square kilometers of unbroken, rugged mountains interrupted here and there by forested valleys and seldom-traveled highways linking a handful of small villages. A land where more people lived a hundred years ago than do today. Where moose and caribou still outnumber people ten to one. Where there is a wolf for every five humans.

The Yukon is a vast mountain wilderness. It occupies the northwest corner of the great western Cordillera – a long chain of high mountain ridges that stretch the length of North and South America. It is hard to stand anywhere in the Yukon and not see a mountain. There are dozens of ranges: the Barn and British Mountains in the far north, the Ruby Range and St. Elias Mountains to the west, the Coast and Cassiar Mountain to the south, and the great backbone of the Selwyn Mountains forming the east boundary of the territory. In between there are many more mountain ranges, big and small.

To the casual eye the mountains are rock and snow, an impossible place for animals to live. But if we look closer we find even the highest plateaus, ridges and slopes support vegetation. There is plant life, and animal food is everywhere on the mountain. And a handful of Yukon herbivores have found ways to thrive in the mountain world. Moose, caribou, and Dall's sheep migrate up and down the slopes in search of seasonal food, cover, insect relief, escape terrain, water, breeding and birthing areas, and other features they need to survive. The mountain supports diverse mammal life and wolves have learned how to hunt it.

There are 5,000 wolves in the Yukon and they live virtually everywhere. They roam the Yukon North Slope following caribou, they cross the highest glaciers of Kluane hunting Dall's sheep and mountain goat, and they work the forested river plateaus preying on moose. The Yukon wolf is a mountain wolf. I can't think of a wolf pack home range that does not include a mountain range. Although the mountains seem impassable to us, the rugged terrain actually makes travel easy for wolves. Using windblown ridges and slopes wolves can move quickly across their territories in all seasons – even in the deepest part of the winter. I have seen wolves move 40 kilometers in a single day using snow-free ridges to travel from one valley to the next and kill a moose. Yukon wolves have learned where, when, and how to hunt and kill mountain prey.

Between 1982 and 2000, I studied wolves in many places in the Yukon. I worked with other biologists, wildlife technicians, students, and pilots. We worked mostly in winter – the season to find the snow trails that led us to wolves. I flew in small planes following snow trails for hundreds of thousands of kilometers through every major watershed in the territory. When I found a pack my team chased wolves down with helicopters and darted them with immobilizing drugs. I placed radiocollars around their necks then spent thousands of hours in airplanes mapping home ranges; studying their reproductive biology; calculating kill rates on moose, Dall's sheep and caribou; and estimating wolf survival rates. I visited their dens and collected scats to understand summer diet. I extracted wolf blood and serum to study disease and genetics.

I also killed wolves by shooting them from aircraft, or I found them and called in helicopter crews who did the killing. We skinned them and performed necropsies on their carcasses. We weighed them; measured body length and height, skull width, and canine length and width. We examined them for broken ribs and leg bones, and aged them by pulling a tooth and counting cementum annuli. We measured fat to assess their physical condition, and examined stomachs and intestines for parasites. I learned everything I could learn about Yukon wolves.

I became an expert on the response of moose, caribou and Dall's sheep to wolf control. I had a keen interest in understanding how wolf populations recover after being greatly reduced. I helped design the first study to examine the effects of fertility-control to arrest wolf reproduction – and replace killing them from helicopters. Through it all, I came to better understand the critical role wolves play in shaping northern ecosystems. And, inevitably, I learned many things about myself. In this section of the book I hope to share some of the things I have come to understand about Yukon wolves. I also hope to shed some new light on this highly successful predator that will challenge the way we have managed them for many decades.

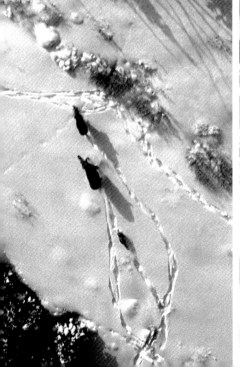

8

Snow

Rogue River – 15 February 1989

It is -25°C outside the plane and not much warmer inside the cockpit. I am bundled in a huge expedition down parka, wearing wind pants over heavy wool pants over long johns. My cool hands are clenched inside woolen mitts. My headset is pulled over a toque pushed down over my ears and forehead. I am wearing winter boots apparently rated to keep my toes warm to -40°C. But I am starting to lose feeling in my left foot, the first unpleasant sign that we have been at this for more than an hour.

Ray Harbats is sitting in front of me. He is the pilot I am training to snowtrack. The little bit of heat that is coming from the engine of the PA-18 Super Cub spills into the cabin in front of him. Ray is wearing thick winter coveralls that form a wall, blocking what little warm air there is from reaching me. I hold my knees in from the frigid sides of the Super Cub. I am hoping for some heat to escape around Ray into the back of the plane but little makes it.

The plexiglas windows are continually frosting from our cool breath. I find my small ice scraper and I work the left window, briefly improving my view of the frozen river below. I see a fresh wolverine trail traveling close to the bank. The wolverine has slipped under fallen trees and eroded banks hoping to surprise a snowshoe hare or grouse. Wolves never travel these places, preferring the open river to move quickly in search of moose.

A large pack killed a moose lower down the river and we have been following it since about 10 a.m. this morning. The trail has disappeared off the river and we are circling the forest to find it again. Rivers are major winter highways for wolves. The snow is always windblown and harder than in the forest making for fast travel. The wolves will likely return to the Rogue River if they haven't killed a moose in the timber below. Ray is shifting from the left to right window checking for tracks as he pilots the plane about a hundred meters above the ground. We are cruising at about eighty-five kilometers per hour; just slow enough to see details in the snow but fast enough to stay safely airborne. Suddenly

the plane is banking sharply to the right. "I got something",
Ray says. I shift to the right window and peer down as he
turns the plane in a tight circle. I see the trail along the
riverbank, but I quickly lose it in the high timber. As we
circle back again I find the trail cutting through high bushes,
then it is back on the river ice. Which way are they going,
and are they going up or down the bank? My voice crackles
over the intercom, "They're going our way. See the leap
marks where the wolves have jumped off the riverbank?
There's a heavy spray of snow at the leading edge of the push
marks. The wolves are still heading upriver." Ray confirms
he sees the sign and we fly ahead.

I continually look below to confirm the track direction.
I think about the many times that wolves doubled back on
their trail, or vanished in heavy moose trails, or the many
kilometers I have flown before realizing I was going the
wrong direction. I have a simple rule that has come from
losing too many wolf trails – I never believe I am following
the tracks in the right direction. That way I will stay focused
on the track details and not be surprised.

I tell Ray to fly a little higher. He pulls back on the
flight stick lifting the plane a few hundred meters above the
river. I am trading off track definition for increased sight
range along both sides of the river. We both look ahead
expecting to see wolves at any moment, but there is only the
snow trail weaving up the river.

The wolves eventually leave the river at a wide bend. I
tell Ray to cut the corner and we meet the river again. The
wolf tracks are still with us. Here the river has overflowed.
The pack trail reaches the ice and divides into individual

tracks and I get my first count of how many wolves are traveling together.

"Six", I say, but I know there are more. Suddenly a web of tracks appears below us heading in every direction. Ray sees the dead moose and calls out, "A kill!" He pulls the stick to the left and banks the plane so I can get a glimpse of the carcass before it passes behind the Super Cub.

The dead moose is near shore – at least what is left of it. The rib cage has been stripped and its legs are mostly eaten. The wolves have torn the hide to pieces and there are long moose hairs scattered around the kill. Ray pulls the throttle back slightly and we are circling low over the moose. I look between the high spruce trees for wolves. There are many trails leading on and off the river but the wolves have gone. We fly lower for a closer inspection of the kill.

"I think it's a bull", I say. I can just make out the pedicels or bony bumps on the side of the bull's skull where his heavy antlers were attached before he dropped them in December. I pull a pencil from inside my mitt and scribble the location on the map. There are many wolverine trails leading to and from the kill. Wolverines visit kills after wolves have left, avoiding any unwelcome confrontations. The pack is somewhere upriver.

There is another icy patch a few kilometers upstream where the trail splits into eight distinct tracks. And there are more clues we are heading the right way. The morning light is bright enough to show foot print details. I can see the four toe marks all pointing upstream. One of the wolves has run a short distance and I can make out the light spray of snow ahead of the tracks where his foot has pushed the shallow snow ahead. We are still going the right way.

We fly along for another ten minutes with the fresh-looking trail beside us. I check my map and guess we have followed the wolves for thirty kilometers or so. We pass over many old and fresh tracks of moose, fox, and snowshoe hare using the river. Then another dead moose appears ahead. We both call into our microphones. Ray kicks the right rudder and circles the Super Cub back over it. The carcass is completely gone and so are the wolves. I figure it to be a calf by the short neck and small skeleton. We fly another dozen kilometers and there is another kill in the middle of the river. It's adult size, but I can't tell for sure. It could be a yearling. We circle through the forest, but still no wolves. Further upstream the trail climbs a low bank and vanishes into heavy timber. We search the surrounding meadows and river channels. Finally, I see it in a heavy moose trail. The wolves' low bellies have sculpted out the edges of the moose tracks. I describe what I am seeing to Ray. He nods but I wonder if he can see the subtle transformation in the moose trail. It took me years to recognize the sign.

A few hundred meters ahead the trail is back on the river. Further ahead the trail leaves and returns to the river many times. They are hunting moose. We are now deep in the headwaters of the Rogue River, about fifty kilometers from the Northwest Territories border where the river forms from the joining of two large mountain creeks. I can see the wolf trail heading for a large meadow between the forks. Then it stops dead. At first I think the tracks have blown in. We fly the edge of the meadow expecting the trail to reappear but there is nothing but soft, trackless snow below. Then I remember my first rule – never believe I am following the tracks in the right direction. "They've stopped and doubled back. They're behind us somewhere."

Through the left window I find the breakout trail heading up the south fork drainage and into a rugged mountain valley. Moose tracks begin to appear everywhere. We pass directly over a cow and calf moose and not far ahead I see running moose trails in the bushes along the creek and wolf leap marks are everywhere I look. The wolf pack suddenly appears weaving in and out of the brush. Five meters ahead is a moose running for its life.

Ray and I call out excitedly, "I got nine, twelve, no fourteen...they're all blacks...pull up...we're disturbing the hunt." We can't stay. The plane accelerates ahead and we climb up above the valley. I look back to see the wolves scattering through the bushes. The moose is still running up the creek then I lose it behind the plane. As the wing lifts I see many moose trails on the high mountain slopes beside us. Ray finds an updraft and the Super Cub climbs slowly up the ridges to the alpine. We fly over three groups of cows with calves standing in waist deep snow a thousand meters above the valley floor. They are not here to feed – they are here to escape the wolves.

We circle back over the valley and I see the wolves far below on the creek. They have come together again and have the moose surrounded. I try to recount them but they are too far away to be sure. We fly out of the mountain valley and head back down the Rogue River. The engine coughs and sputters briefly as Ray switches to the right wing fuel tank. "Time to head home," he says. "Good tracking job, Ray. That was a lot of fun", I reply. He has learned quickly, and has had lots of opportunities to track wolves. The upper Stewart

River basin is a rich moose-wolf ecosystem. We have tracked a dozen or more packs together in the last week. It is the most impressive moose range I have ever seen, with a fantastic mosaic of large burns, climax spruce forests, rivers, and high mountains. I find the pencil with my cold fingers and awkwardly scribble '14 black wolves' and add the moose sightings on the map. I measure the wolf trail at roughly one hundred kilometers. Anticipating a rather boring direct flight back to camp, I am suddenly aware of how cold I am. I settle into the hard seat, adjust the pillow under me, and tuck my mitts into the pockets of my parka. I have now lost all feeling in my left foot.

En route home I spot eight wolves standing in the middle of Fairweather Lake in heavy caribou trails. We drop down to get a closer look. I count one light cream, three grays and five blacks. We circle a few times then leave them, knowing we will never figure out where they came from with all the caribou sign. We cut over to the South Macmillan River and fly up Russell Creek. We stay low over the trees and begin our descent to Moose Lake and our field camp. Then I realize I can't hear the Super Cub's engine. I look up at Ray and he seems to be unconcerned, so I think he must have pulled the power back to glide down to the lake. We are barely skimming over the treetops when we reach the lakeshore. The plane glides down to the lake and the skis touch down in the deep snow. We stop, barely one hundred meters away from the shore. The propeller is not moving.

"The engine quit!" Ray exclaims as he turns to me. We have been having some trouble flying on the right tank but have never lost the engine before. He plays with the gas line switch and turns the key. The engine roars to life. Our strip

is a few kilometers on the other side of Moose Lake. "Let's
not bother flying", I suggest and Ray nods agreeably. We taxi
through the deep snow across the lake and park next to our
fuel cache. It is lunchtime, and the smoke billowing from the
cabin's chimney means I will be warm once again.

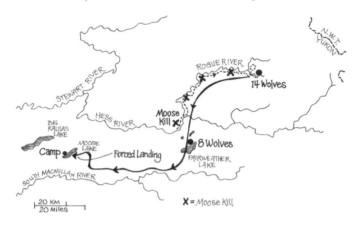

A lan Baer is the Yukon's wolf technician and he worked
with me on all aspects of the wolf program for eighteen
years. He and I conducted wolf counts together in
sixteen areas searching a grand total of 750,000 square-
kilometers of snowy country. We surveyed some areas many
times including the 25,000 square-kilometer Finlayson wolf
study area for thirteen years, the 12,000 square-kilometer
Coast Mountains for six years, and the 20,000 square-
kilometer Aishihik study area for nine years. We counted
wolves in all regions of the Yukon.

We found some interesting things about wolves and what
drives their numbers. First and foremost, Yukon wolf
abundance is closely linked to moose numbers. Wolves are
least numerous in the northern Yukon where moose are lightly

scattered through the Arctic taiga, and in the high mountains of the Kluane region where wolves prey mainly on the elusive and small Dall's sheep. The best wolf populations are in the central and southern Yukon where moose and woodland caribou are relatively abundant. Second, we found wolf territories were more or less similar in size in all areas but pack size was linked to moose. Wolf pack size is ultimately regulated by the survival of pups. And the more moose the pack kills the greater the chance the pups will survive their first winter. In low moose areas wolf packs are often less than four or five wolves, with only one or two pups. In good moose areas packs of 10-15 wolves are common, with six or seven pups traveling in the group.

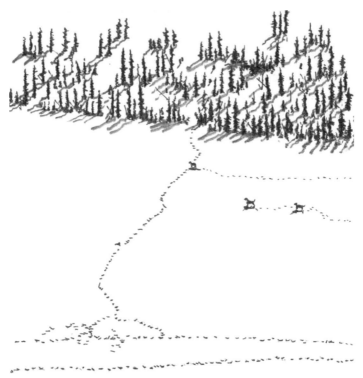

Our abilities to find wolves improved as we learned to tell their tracks from wolverine, coyote, and fox. We learned how to follow wolves through forests full of moose and caribou tracks, and track them through Dall's sheep trails along the high mountain ridges. We became familiar with the shapes and sizes of many different animals tracks, what they look like under different snow and light conditions, and the subtle clues showing direction of travel.

In the early years there were many hard tracking lessons, some humorous. We followed wolverine tracks long distances before recognizing the shorter steps in their trails. I followed a 'wolf' trail forty kilometers up the Ketza Road near Ross River only to find a musher and his dog team at the end of it. We both spent many hours tracking wolf trails backwards, eventually realizing our error when the tracks became increasingly snow-covered.

Caribou trails are the most difficult to follow wolves through. Like wolves, caribou form narrow trails and will travel many kilometers before stopping to feed or rest. When wolves enter caribou trails they can follow them for many kilometers without breaking off. To the untrained eye it seems the wolves have vanished. But the tracks are there. It takes good light conditions and concentration to see how the shorter wolves smooth out and flatten the snow between the caribou tracks.

Under ideal conditions I could follow wolf trails even through heavily tracked caribou range. One of my most memorable snowtracking events was on the Yukon North Slope in April 1987. We found a freshly killed caribou and wolf tracks heading off the Babbage River. The tundra of the North Slope is typically windblown so it is rare to be able to follow tracks of any animal very far. That spring the weather was calm after a heavy snowfall. We followed the wolf pack east into the Barn Mountains where thousands of Porcupine caribou were migrating. The trail was easy to follow until it vanished in a large caribou feeding area. The caribou had already moved on, and it was impossible to find the wolf tracks among the thousands of craters and caribou prints. We circled the perimeter of the feeding area until we found where the wolf trail left. We followed it through the mountains to the next feeding area. We spent a few hours tracking the wolves this way discovering three caribou kills they made. We ran low on fuel and had to return to our field camp in Old Crow.

We returned the next day and continued where we left off. Eventually the wolves turned and headed back to the Babbage River where we had started our tracking the day before. After three more caribou kills we found the wolves – four black and two grays – resting on a ridge, only a few hundred meters from their first kill on the Babbage River. The wolf trail was eighty kilometers long and formed a full circle showing a week of their caribou hunting lives.

There was another memorable tracking event – this time in a helicopter. In 1987 I helped Peter Clarkson, then the Northwest Territories wolf biologist, collar his first wolves in the Bluenose caribou range east of Inuvik. On 20 March we were flying in a Jet Ranger helicopter heading to Peter's field camp at Husky Lakes. Below us were hundreds of heavy caribou trails. The day was clear and ideal for snowtracking. I began to casually study the various trails winding across the tundra. Then I recognized a fresh wolf trail following caribou. I told the pilot to drop down for a closer look. He was skeptical that anyone could tell the difference between animal tracks from so high in the air. We descended to where I could clearly make out the fresh prints of two wolves joining a 10-meter wide caribou trail heading west. We landed and I filled some darts with drug and pushed one down into the gun barrel. We followed the caribou trail until I saw where the wolves left and headed to a low ridge. As we flew ahead the tracks changed from walking to running, then leaping; and I knew the wolves had heard us coming. Seconds later we flew over the wolves. I darted them both and Peter had his first Bluenose wolves radiocollared and on the air before we arrived at camp.

Snowtracking requires two essential qualities: excellent eyesight and an aversion to being airsick. The rest of it can be learned. A typical day of snowtracking is five to six hours of intense flying in a low level circling motion. While constantly watching for the subtle clues of direction and wolf activity, you can't get airsick. Fortunately both Alan and I could handle the constant spinning, twisting, and yawing of the small planes without getting vertigo. But many others who wanted to work with wolves soon gave up after a few hours of feeling terribly ill.

My wolf studies could never have happened without highly skilled and keenly interested fixed-wing pilots. I trained various pilots, including Ray Harbats – the pilot in the narrative – Hans Lammers, Jim Buerge, and Rob Pyde. But there were four key pilots who did most of the tracking: Tom Hudgin, Denny Denison and two brothers, Derek and Cam Drinnan. I spent nearly ten years flying with Tom sharing nearly 3,000 hours in his PA-18 Super Cub. Tom learned how to fly in his father's aviation business in the fabled Grand Canyon of Arizona. As a teenager he was already flying the rugged canyons and coulees where winds and ground thermals left him no room for mistakes. Tom is a natural-born pilot, but he continually practiced his mountain flying skills in the Yukon. On many return flights to our field camp at Rose Lake near Whitehorse, Tom would descend over the top of Primrose Mountain, cut the engine and drop silently into an impossibly steep and narrow canyon before finally leveling the plane and quietly settling onto the landing strip on the frozen lake.

The Super Cub seemed an extension of Tom – or he was an organic part of the plane. Tom rarely needed to check his air speed or elevation when we were spinning and twisting a hundred meters above wolf tracks. Tom always kept his eyes on the ground while he shifted from the left to right window expertly circling the Super Cub over tracks. I asked him how he knew what the plane was doing without constantly checking his instruments. He said he felt the plane through his seat. Besides, he said, joking, he was too busy following the tracks. I flew thousands of hours behind him and I never once felt in danger – even though most of those flying hours were low level, near stall speed, and many kilometers away from camp. We worked well as a team, but Tom did not need me to find wolves. In March 1989, he spent an afternoon tracking wolves alone in the heavily forested plateaus in the Finlayson area in the east central Yukon. By the end of the day Tom found four new wolf packs – a Yukon snowtracking record.

On May 29, 1990, Tom crashed his Single Otter on takeoff near Pelly Crossing. As the big plane descended into the trees the fuel lines were stripped away and the plane was engulfed in flames before it slammed into the ground. Somehow Tom and his assistant escaped from the cockpit, but both suffered first-degree burns. After the crash Tom returned to fly with me but his scarred hands were sensitive to cold. He stopped wolf flying a few years later. I was always grateful for the time we spent in the Super Cub together. Tom still flies for a small aviation company in Whitehorse.

Denny Denison flew a Maule LR-7 airplane. It is a compact and light four-passenger plane that flies faster than the Super Cub. His flying and snowtracking skills were equal to Tom's. The Maule has a higher stall speed than the Super Cub and the side-to-side seating made wolf tracking a different challenge. I sat in the right front seat beside Denny making it difficult for me to see out the left window of the plane. Whenever Denny crossed a wolf trail he always banked the plane to his side so he could follow it out the left window. To see anything I would have to peer over his shoulder. Feeling of little use I'd sometimes say, "I'm paying for the flight – circle the plane on my side for a little while." After I had a brief look Denny continued tracking the wolves from his side.

Denny had an uncanny skill recognizing wolf trails and immediately know which way they were heading. I could never understand what he was seeing so clearly that I couldn't, but it happened too many times to be random luck. Denny' s eyesight was exceptional, and I think he could see details in the snow better than anyone else. But Denny was more than just a good snowtracking pilot. He was keenly interested in wolves and knew as much about their wild behavior as I did. In 1994, I was attending graduate school and could not be present for the first week of my field research. Denny knew the distribution and movement patterns of my radiocollared packs as well as I did. I asked him to schedule the relocations of a dozen packs to determine kill rates until I could get to the field. When I pulled into camp two weeks later the field study was well underway and I did not need to change the schedules.

Denny's keen interest in my research sometimes went beyond the call of duty. In March 1984, Denny and I set neck snares out to live capture wolves near the village of Teslin in the southern Yukon. We flew the area every few days checking for captured wolves. Late one morning we found a wolf caught in a set a few hundred meters from Snafu Lake. Denny landed the Maule along the shore. I loaded two darts, collected the gun from the back seat, and slipped a radio-collar in the darting kit. As we approached the set I could see we had snared a nervous pup. But it had wrapped itself around the anchor tree and was hanging dangerously by its neck. Live snares are built with a metal stop clamped inside the noose that stops the snare from closing tight. But a wolf could still hang itself if a snare is too high from the ground. The pup began to struggle to escape. I moved forward trying not to panic it. I stopped three meters away and fired the dart hitting the wolf in the leg. It instantly panicked and slowly began to go unconscious in the snare. I lowered the rifle sights to see Denny pulling at the snare around the wolf's neck. I ran in and we lifted the wolf out of the snare. Denny dropped to his knees and began to blow into the wolf's mouth then he began pumping on the wolf's diaphragm. After some time, I took over but we failed to save the pup. Few people will do mouth-to-mouth resuscitation on a person – let alone on a wild wolf.

Denny was with me when we snowtracked the largest pack I have ever followed. In March 1992 we were on the Black River, a tributary of the upper Liard River. I saw a wide trail that I thought at first must be a large group of caribou traveling the river. The trail entered a steep canyon. We followed for a few kilometers. At some places the entire river was covered in prints, which began to look more and more like wolves. Denny was quietly thinking the same thing. We both shouted out when we flew by a black wolf lying dead on the ice. The huge wolf trail continued for another twenty kilometers down the Black River canyon. I was able to count forty separate trails in a few places. The wolves eventually turned downstream on the Liard River. We were tempted to follow, but did not have enough fuel. About two weeks later a trapper nearby watched thirty-nine wolves cross the lake in front of his cabin. These large packs are likely a temporary joining of two or more neighboring packs with related adult wolves. These mega packs do not last long due to the intense, natural aggression that exists among the wolves. Before I saw the Black River wolf trail I was skeptical of the reports of large packs of up to fifty wolves in the southern lakes area during the 1950s. I think such large packs existed, at least temporarily.

Derek and Cam Drinnan owned Black Sheep Aviation and Cattle Company. Both brothers learned to fly Super Cubs as young teenagers near Hudson's Hope in northern British Columbia. Both worked as hunting guides before coming to the Yukon in the 1980s. They already knew a lot about wolves, and how to track them in winter. Both Derek and Cam worked with me in the 1990s flying in the Ruby Range Mountains – one of the windiest and difficult places to fly in the Yukon. During winter there are intense storms from the Gulf of Alaska that produce high winds as the low-pressure systems pass over the St. Elias Mountains. These powerful mountain winds touch down in the Ruby Range, blowing away the snow and obliterating fresh tracks in a few seconds. When tracking in these difficult conditions Derek would say it was getting 'ropey' – originally a nautical wind warning that sailors should tie to ropes to work open decks. This was his gentle code for saying the flying was about to get bumpy, and we should think about heading home and snowtrack another day. Cam and Derek had to fly with outmost care as we worked out wolf trails that would inevitably disappear onto a wind-blasted mountain ridge. We often searched the same mountain valley again and again before we found wolves. There were some packs that we never did find even after a few years of intense snowtracking. Derek was caught alone twice in severe turbulence. Both times he was tossed upside down before he could pull the Super Cub out of a stall and recover power.

Over time we got better at tracking down wolves. In the early years we found about 20 percent of the packs we snowtracked. By the end we found most of the packs we tracked, although we often spent one or more days working out the sign. I was reluctant to give up on tracks unless conditions became hopeless in windblown mountains or dense forests full of moose or caribou trails. Knowing when to stay or give up on a wolf trail only came with experience. However, once we found wolves we needed a way to keep in contact with them to understand their role they played in the Yukon wilderness.

9

Capture

Tyers River – 2 March 1990

The turbine of the Jet Ranger helicopter ignites and the long blades slowly rotate above us. Soon the engine is roaring and the main rotor is turning quickly. A torrent of blinding snow enshrouds the helicopter. The radiocollared wolf is ten meters away and I can see he is beginning to recover from the drugging. He lifts his head and looks vacantly at us. The Telazol is blocking the nerve pathways to his muscles and his mind is still foggy. He is temporarily immobile and will not be able to move his legs for another twenty minutes. But he looks fine and should be safe from any raven that should happen by. I am confident about leaving him here. He lays his head back down then disappears in the blowing snow as the helicopter prepares to leave the high mountain cirque.

Pilot John Witham's voice fills the intercom. "Everybody ready?" Alan Baer is busy locking up the shooting window. "All set", he replies. The Jet Ranger lifts out of the deep snow and moves slowly ahead along the mountain ridge. In a few seconds we rise above the ridge and the Tyers River valley appears below us. The second wolf is somewhere down there.

I reach for the drug kit between my legs and pull out three aluminum dart tubes. I unscrew the 1¼ inch barbed needles from the tube cylinders. I find the vial of Telazol and a hypodermic syringe in the drug kit. I jab the needle through the rubber seal of the vial and draw nine milliliters of the opaque liquid into the syringe. Then I load three milliliters of the drug into each tube, screw the dart needles back onto the tubes, and squeeze a few drops of Vaseline on each needle to keep the drug from leaking out. Alan reaches over my shoulder and takes the darts.

The female wolf has had a 45-minute head start while we collared her mate. This is the first year of the recovery of the Finlayson wolf population after seven years of intensive aerial control. Colonizing wolves are the core of the recovery. Collaring both the male and female is necessary to understand how new pairs behave, reproduce and repopulate the Finlayson area.

The snow is soft, slowing her down and leaving a deep trail to follow. In a few minutes she comes in view running downhill but still above timberline. I watch her lope easily through the snow, and recognize the distinct features of a female wolf. She is smaller bodied and her head is narrower than her sleeping mate on the mountain above us. She ploughs smoothly and efficiently through the deep snow.

John needs no instruction. He has collared more than a hundred wolves. He flies over the black wolf and hovers a few hundred meters below her, blocking her escape into the forested valley. She turns uphill and moves back up the mountain on her deep trail – exactly where we want her. A rush of cold air fills the cockpit as Alan slides his shooting window open. His voice crackles above the wind rushing through his microphone.

"Ready...she's small so I only want to use one dart", Alan says. He is holding the gun inside the cockpit, covering the breech with his gloved hand to keep the dart from freezing. He has removed the glove on his right hand, his bare finger resting on the trigger guard.

The wolf stops and looks back watching the thundering helicopter approach. We are five meters away when she begins to leap uphill. So far it is a textbook darting. John swings the nose of the helicopter slightly left giving Alan a wide view of the escaping wolf. Alan leans out the window and raises the gun to his right shoulder. The wolf is under the rotor now where the dart will not be affected by blade turbulence. But just as Alan is about to fire, the wolf turns and runs straight for the helicopter and disappears under us.

"Damn..." shouts Alan in the crackling microphone, "...no shot." The wolf is below us heading for the timber.

John slides the Jet Ranger sideways past her, down the mountain. Then he pulls the machine into a hover over some small alpine fir trees. The wolf heads straight at us, no longer afraid of the noisy machine. We cannot hold her as she slips under us again and again down the forested slope. She is smart and won't be coaxed uphill a second time. I begin looking below for openings in the trees where we can dart her.

She continues loping smoothly through the trees until she reaches the valley bottom. I can see she is tiring as she begins to walk through the dense forest. She crosses a small opening in the forest and disappears under a large spruce tree. We hover above waiting for her to move but after a minute she still hasn't appeared. John carefully takes the machine down the side of the big tree blowing snow to push her out. The wash from the main rotor blades knocks the snow from the branches. John climbs back up, and as we rise above the trees I look for the wolf running below. But there is no wolf. John circles the big tree again and again. We circle around the nearby trees but there is no trail anywhere. She is still under the big spruce tree.

"Can you land?" I ask John. "I'll get out and try to move her." There is a small opening in the forest a few hundred meters away. John circles sizing up the distance between the high trees. Satisfied there is room for the rotors, he slowly takes the helicopter down through the trees and the machine settles on the deep snow. Alan passes me the dart gun and darts and says, "I'll cover you." He is grinning, patting the handgun tucked under his jacket. I only nod at his joke and remove my headset.

I climb out under the spinning blades, carefully shifting my weight to avoid tilting the helicopter which is hovering under full power, its belly settled precariously on the soft snow. I move to the back of the machine and open the storage compartment, pull out a pair of snowshoes, and close the door. Kneeling beside the skid, I cover my face as the helicopter lifts off. I strap on the snowshoes and begin walking to the tree. The snow is soft and the snowshoes sink to my mid thigh. After only fifty meters I am already breathing heavily.

While the helicopter circles above I slowly approach the tree. I expect to see the wolf running away any second. I peer cautiously into the heavy lower branches but there is nothing moving. I look to the helicopter, shake my head, and shrug my shoulders. The helicopter moves off and begins flying above the surrounding forest. I push the heavy branches back and look carefully. Her fresh prints disappear down a hole in the snow beside the tree trunk. I stop and move back a few meters. She is right here. My heart races as I check for my handgun holstered under my arm. I try to peer down the hole, expecting to see the wolf staring up at me. As I move closer I can see the thick branches of a fallen tree a few meters below. She's down there hiding under the tree trunk. I kneel and listen carefully for movement but hear nothing.

I consider what to do. I lean the dart gun against the tree and take my snowshoes off. I start digging with a snowshoe into the soft snow around the hole. In a few minutes I have dug down two meters to reach the fallen tree. As I dig I realize the wolf is trapped in a snow tunnel and cannot escape without first crawling out through the branches. I am safe I think – at least for now.

The helicopter returns and hovers above me. I climb out from my excavation, pointing down to the snow. Alan opens his window and looks puzzled. I shout up, "She's gone under the snow." He nods and the helicopter flies to where they dropped me off. I continue shoveling another ten minutes until I am standing in a trench about three meters long and two meters deep. I am slowly uncovering the fallen tree.

While I dig I stop often to listen. I can hear the soft shuffling somewhere below but I still have not seen the wolf. As the trench grows she keeps moving further down along the tree. Alan appears above me, exhausted and sweating. He has shed his heavy winter parka after wading through the chest-deep snow. He peers down at me and asks coyly, "What are you digging for?"

"She's working her way under the tree", I answer as I push down on the thick trunk with my foot. Alan takes the other snowshoe and slides into the trench. After twenty minutes the trench is four meters long. The wolf is running out of room to hide and we can hear her shuffling nervously under us. Then a faint shout comes from far way in the forest. It is John. "It is getting dark, we gotta go." I look at Alan. It is late afternoon and the setting sun is casting dark shadows making it hard to see under the fallen tree. Alan shakes his head. "Keep digging", he says. We drive our snowshoes into the snow with determined haste.

Then I see a patch of dark fur move slightly. I wave to Alan and point silently into the branches. I climb out of the trench and grab the dart gun. I find the dart in my jacket, load it in the rifle, and aim. In the low light I am not sure what part of the wolf I am aiming for. I fire hoping the dart will not hit the spine. The wolf shuffles noisily for a few minutes then it stops moving. We stand quietly. The Telazol is working. Alan takes the pointed tail of his snowshoe and gently prods at the wolf.

"She's out", he whispers. He climbs under the tree, and reaches down. He gently pulls her limp body up through the tangle of branches to me. The dart has hit her square on the rump – a perfect, and perfectly lucky shot. Alan is beaming. "A hell of a shot", he says. He scrambles out of the trench. I feel under the crotch and confirm it is a female. I gently open her mouth. The canine teeth are slightly worn and barely discolored. Her face hair is jet black with no gray on the muzzle. She is a young adult wolf, maybe two years old. I lift her body above my shoulders wedging it against the snow trench. Alan reaches down and pulls her up and away. As she disappears, I see the light is nearly gone in the trees. John's distant voice breaks the shadowy silence again. We will be flying home in the dark.

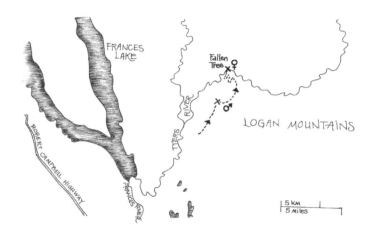

R adiotelemetry was essential for studying wild Yukon wolves. To understand their biology, I had to observe them and to do so on a regular basis, again and again. Capturing them was the first – and trickiest – step in the study process.

To capture a wolf requires exact coordination between a highly skilled helicopter pilot and a darting expert sitting behind him. Shooting a running wolf with a dart fired from a moving helicopter involves unpredictable and sudden 3-dimensional changes in the angle of the rifle barrel, and the constantly changing distance to the moving target. Add in the moving target is intelligent and will stop, swerve away, dash behind a tree, or bolt under the machine to avoid capture. I worked with two wildlife technicians, Philip Merchant and Alan Baer, who over the years, became the expert darters. Each developed a supreme patience waiting for the shoulder or hind end of a fast running wolf to appear at just the right moment before squeezing the trigger.

I worked with Philip when I first started studying wolves. In the spring of 1987, Philip and I chased a pair of wolves along the headwaters of the Firth River in the northern Yukon. The first one he darted was a male. It ran into a long string of small and steep hills, constantly dodging under spruce trees for cover. Philip leaned out the rear door waiting for the right moment to shoot. Suddenly, the wolf stopped. The pilot pulled the helicopter in a hover just as the wolf made a 180^0 turn to escape in the opposite direction. Philip leaned back and with one hand he aimed the dart gun and shot the wolf in the rump from six meters away. It was a difficult shot to make with two steady hands – a near impossible shot fired upside down with one hand.

Darting the female was less easy but even more exciting. She was elusive – spinning, twisting, and turning to avoid the thundering helicopter as we made a half dozen unsuccessful passes over her. To reduce our weight we landed and I climbed out of the helicopter and waited on the ground. Within a few minutes the helicopter appeared flying low over the wolf about 500 meters away. From where I stood it looked as if the wolf was on a line as it bobbed up and down under the skids jumping up to bite at the helicopter. Then it somehow hooked on the skids with its forelegs. It hung there for some seconds before falling to the ground. Then the wolf and helicopter disappeared. Ten minutes later the pilot returned and picked me up. We flew to Philip who was a kilometer away in a meadow, kneeling over the sleeping female wolf. While we fixed the collar on, Philip recounted how he and the wolf faced each other a meter away. He had no shot, he said, seeing only the flashing canines of the invited passenger on the helicopter skid.

Wolf darting takes place during a dangerous, high-speed chase. The art of darting is to predict the physics of motion in the intervening second between pulling the trigger and the dart contacting the moving wolf. This all happens too fast to carefully calculate. Imagine you are in the back seat of a helicopter flying two meters off the ground going forty kilometers per hour. Everything in front of you is going by in a blur: trees, rocks, ground cover. But you must focus on the wolf running just ahead of the helicopter skids, and trust the pilot with the rest. You wait until the ground conditions, speed, distance and the target are all momentarily fixed in relative space – a millisecond. The wolf is coming inside the rotor wash. You lean out and aim into the space slightly ahead of the running wolf, knowing the dart will travel slowly through the air in a shallow arc and meet the wolf's thigh muscle. In this perfect moment the wolf could stop or swerve under the helicopter and the dart will fly harmlessly into the ground.

Alan Baer worked with me as the Yukon wolf technician for nearly two decades. He darted hundreds of wolves. When I hired him in 1983, he was already an excellent rifleman, having honed his skills target shooting and hunting since he was a teenager. Alan's first time darting was in 1984 when we chased a pack through the Coast Mountains south of Whitehorse. We separated a young wolf from the pack and slowly moved it onto a steep alpine mountain slope – a perfect spot for learning to dart. Unfortunately, it was very windy and the pilot was also a first-timer, reluctant to fly low. Alan was having trouble adapting his competition shooting skills to the much slower speed of the dart. After the first few shots went behind the wolf I imprudently chose to give him advice. From the look he gave me, I quickly saw that I was only making him more nervous, so I shut up. With each subsequent pass Alan was too high or did not lead the wolf far enough. The dart supply diminished rapidly until I was holding the last one in my hand.

"This is it", I said – trying to sound relaxed. I handed it to him. He was shaken and asked if I wanted to take over. I said, "No, go ahead...you'll hit it this time." The dart flew harmlessly into the snow then the wolf disappeared over the mountain. For years after we jokingly referred to the area as 'sleepy mountain'.

Despite his unremarkable debut, Alan became a formidable expert at capturing wolves. After that first day he rarely missed a shot. Alan immobilized dozen of wolves each winter, often using only a single dart on each capture. Like Philip, Alan took great care to not endanger the wolf and would never get flustered if the pilots wondered aloud why he hadn't made a shot. "It's not right", was his easy reply from the shooting window. Better no wolf than an injured one.

On February 1993 I watched how good Alan was at wolf darting. From the backseat of a plane I followed behind the helicopter as it pursued a pack of eight wolves running over a narrow lake. The excited wolves splintered into three groups that strung out along the lake. I watched the helicopter slip in low behind the trailing group. I saw Alan lean out the right rear door and methodically dart one wolf in each group as the helicopter made a single pass over the lake. It all happened in less than a minute. All three wolves were lying unconscious on the lake ice ten minutes later. But Alan and Philip could not have been successful at darting without remarkable pilots in the front seat.

The 'right' helicopter pilot is also essential to the capture process. To capture wolves, the helicopter must be taken to the safe operating limits of the machinery. There is a fine line between the pilots who are comfortable pushing the envelope safely and those who are not. Overcautious pilots fly too high or too slow to keep on target with running wolves. The good ones are more than expert flyers – they are instinctive and become part of the flying machine. Once a chase begins and the helicopter is thundering along a few meters off the ground, only the daring pilots will invent the right darting opportunities for the gunner behind. Obstacles such as trees, deadfall, high bush, cliffs, and rising mountain slopes leave no room for mistakes. The pilot must be instantly and always aware of where the main and tail rotors are spinning in relation to the ground.

There are also many environmental factors that affect how the helicopter will perform. With higher-altitude pursuits, the power and control of the helicopter falls dramatically. Subtle changes in wind strength and direction affect performance more at high altitude than in the low valleys. In the thin, high mountain air, the flight controls turn mushy and the machine is much slower to react to the pilot's actions. Because the chase rarely follows an ideal flight path, winds from behind or strong downdrafts from above can suddenly compromise essential lift needed for these high-power, 'red-line' maneuvers. To fly safely, the good pilots possess an instantaneous feel and a Zen-like understanding of the effects of wind and elevation on helicopter performance.

To make it more challenging, mix in the elements of the rapidly changing mountain terrain, the slope of the ground, and the unpredictable shifts in wind velocity and direction.

The wolf's speed and direction can suddenly change if it is moving up or down steep mountains, through trees, over boulders and fallen trees, and through changing snow depth and hardness. The danger to the flight crew is obvious, but the wolf is also at great risk. If the helicopter is too low the target is the wolf's side. Here the dart may penetrate the ribs puncturing vital organs in the gut, killing the wolf. If the shot is from directly over the back, the dart may sever the spinal chord.

Not all pilots made good wolf jockeys, and I could quickly tell the ones that did because they loved the chase. A handful of men stand out for their flying abilities and their wolf pursuit skills. Philip Merchant and I began working with John Fletcher and Matt Conant in 1983 in the rugged terrain of the Coast Mountains where strong winter winds battered us almost daily. Our early darting flights were often in difficult and dangerous mountain conditions. Both John and Matt flew us safely, creating the right opportunities to capture fifty-four wolves. John was tragically electrocuted while repairing a sign near the Alaska Highway in the late 1980s. Matt still flies helicopters. Norman Graham and Jim Hodges captured fifty-one wolves in the north Yukon. Both possess a calm coolness that made darting flights especially smooth and comfortable. But John Witham and Doug Makkonen piloted most of our wolf capture flights and I knew their skills the best.

Both John and Doug flew their helicopters differently. John was an aggressive pursuit pilot. He developed his skills as part of the wolf control team that shot wolves through the 1980s in the Finlayson area. John was an exceptional snowtracker, able to follow wolf trails through dense forest filled with caribou tracks and feeding craters. He was most skilled at knowing how to herd wolves into small forest openings for darting attempts. Less experienced pilots tried to push the wolves too hard, flying close behind them over the trees. Inevitably the wolves would panic and escape in all directions, spoiling any dart opportunity. John would hover far behind the wolves, sometimes more than a kilometer away. The wolves remained calm, apparently thinking they were escaping the bothersome helicopter. By slowly flying back and forth above the trees, John could move a pack many kilometers through thick boreal forest to a tiny opening or meadow. The moment the wolves entered the opening John flew in low over the trees and dropped onto the surprised wolves. The helicopter was always perfectly positioned so that the wolves were just below Alan's shooting window. Alan often had only a second or two to aim and fire before John hauled the helicopter out of the opening to avoid hitting the trees.

But if John Witham flew his Bell 206 Jet Ranger like a hard riding Harley-Davidson motorcycle, Doug Makkonen flew his like it was a smooth riding Cadillac sedan. Doug was my favorite chase pilot because he always made it feel like the captures were easy even in difficult conditions. He is a natural-born pilot with uncanny technical skills and complete knowledge of the aerodynamics of helicopter flight. Legend has it that after his first check-out flight, the chief pilot climbed out of the Bell 47 helicopter, shrugged and said, "He's a way better pilot than I am." On Doug's first wolf darting flight he was flying too high above a wolf running through a broad snow covered meadow. I told him to drop down a little lower. We made a second pass, this time barely above the low bushes. There was a soft thud under the skids and I looked back to see the surprised wolf rolling through the deep snow. "Is that low enough?" Doug asked innocently.

Doug was especially good in severe winds. I flew with him on many captures in the Ruby Range Mountains when most other pilots would decline and wait for a calmer day. On December 20, 1997, I snowtracked a pack of eight wolves along the Kaskawulsh River in Kluane National Park, eventually locating them high on Hoodoo Mountain on a fresh moose kill. It was too late to try capturing one, but by the next morning high winds were blowing in the Park. Doug was still confident he could get us in to dart a wolf. Park warden Terry Skjonsberg and I climbed into the helicopter and we flew back to Hoodoo Mountain into the gusty headwinds. The wolves were scattered along a high ridge on the downwind side of the mountain. I remember thinking that staying airborne – never mind darting – would be impossible in those winds. Terry prepared a dart and said he was ready. I looked down at a huge swirling tower of snow cascading up the ridge and told him to prepare a few extra darts because things were going to get tough quickly. Terry hesitated saying it was a Parks Canada protocol to prepare a single dart at a time. Doug interrupted saying, "If you want to go down there you better have a handful ready." Huge columns of snow spun off the mountain peaks and swirled along the ridges as we approached the wolves. In a near whiteout Doug pushed one, then two, then three wolves up the wind blasted slopes as Terry expertly darted them.

After more than thirty years of flying, Doug is still considered among the very best mountain pilots in the world. He performed many daring high elevation rescues in the St. Elias Mountains near Haines Junction, plucking imperiled climbers from ridges his Jet Ranger helicopter could barely fly to, let alone operate safely. In 2002 he won the coveted Robert E. Trimble Memorial Award for a series of rescues that defied both gravity and physics. With a huge alpine storm coming in Doug repeatedly flew to a high camp of desperate climbers, plucking them one by one off Mount Logan, the highest peak in Canada.

I believe there are no better helicopters pilots flying anywhere in the world than those that flew wolf captures. Without their exceptional flying skills I would not have radiocollared so many wolves. My crews captured 383 wolves between 1983 and 2000. Of those, only four wolves died from the capture process. I often look back in wonder that we never crashed a helicopter or caused injury to a member of the flight crew during darting. It is a testimony to the combined skills of the dart gunners and pilots – and certainly some good luck.

But capturing the wolf was only the beginning. Once the wolf was immobilized, we attached a radiocollar around its neck. The half-kilogram collar enclosed a tiny battery-powered transmitter protected inside a sealed container. Each transmitter was a unique radio frequency that identified the individual wolf. We used airplanes equipped with a special receiver to locate the signals. The receiver was connected to a directional antenna mounted on the plane's wing struts. Under good conditions I could hear the faint beeping signal of a collared wolf from as far away as fifty kilometers. The strength of the signal increased as the plane got closer so I could quickly isolate which side of the plane the wolf was on. Once I was above the wolf I could see what it was doing and my understanding of the biology of Yukon wolves began.

The collars helped us answer interesting questions about the ecology of Yukon wolves that had not been studied before. My main interest was to better understand how wolf predation affected Yukon big game populations. Before we began our studies there was almost nothing known about how often wolves killed moose, caribou, or Dall's sheep. Before collars, we did not know which age classes of prey were most vulnerable, or if wolves killed more males than females.

Using radiocollars, we calculated how many and what type of prey wolves killed in winter. Over the years, we followed seventy-five different wolf packs every day for weeks – and sometimes months – recording the species, age and sex of their kills. The research provided never-before collected information about how often different size packs killed these big game animals. By 2000, we amassed more information about wolf kill rates than all other wolf studies combined.

Radiotelemetry also provided a way to keep track of wolves year-round. Over the course of my studies, we found over one hundred wolf dens, documenting pup production and survival. I collected scats from dens to find out what they were killing in summer. Without radiocollars, finding active dens in summer would have been like searching for the proverbial needle in a haystack.

Radiocollars were the only way to study the life histories of Yukon wolves. We learned how long a pup stayed in a pack; when and where it dispersed; how its social status changed; when it died and where; and what killed it. We followed the lives of hundreds of collared wolves over the years and found nearly all died before they reached four years. Most times other wolves killed them. Other causes included grizzly bears, starvation, avalanche, falling from cliffs, people, and moose.

Faced with killing a moose once a week, the odds of being killed or injured inevitably increase in the constant life and death struggle with this dangerous prey.

Collars also helped us understand the boundaries of wolf pack territories and the places they preferred to hunt in their home ranges. Without radiocollars, I would not have been able to follow the annual recovery of the wolf populations after lethal control ended in three areas of the Yukon. Using radiocollars, graduate student Christie Spence documented how fertility-control reduced wolf reproduction and affected their survival and breeding behavior. Christie's research was the first of its kind on wild free-ranging wolves.

Radiotelemetry gave me the window I needed to look more deeply into wolf behavior and ecology in a vast Yukon wilderness. With the help of expert pilots and technicians, I was able to study the life histories of hundreds of Yukon wolves. Through my research I learned many new things about how they use their environment and how they interact with moose, caribou, Dall's sheep, bears and ravens.

10

The Perfect Prey

Fourth of July Creek – 10 February 1994

T he female is leading her pack along the steep hill. She heads straight up pushing her body through the deep snow. She reaches the top and enters a thick stand of tall spruce trees. The ten other wolves follow close behind, careful to stay in her deep trail. The strong scent of moose suddenly fills her nostrils and she pushes her nose on the hard packed snow searching for the smell. She finds a pile of still-wet moose droppings and gingerly presses her nose into it. They are loose and warm and filled with the scent of calf. Her tail wags as her excitement grows. The other wolves crowd together as they arrive on the moose snow beds. They also shove their noses down and begin sniffing. Soon all the wolves are wagging their tails. The female finds the fresh tracks leading out of the spruce trees and follows it to a large meadow. The scent is much stronger now. The moose are close. She stops to listen but there is only the sound of a light wind blowing through the willow branches. She raises her tail and her mate falls in behind her as the rest of pack enters the meadow.

The cow moose senses there is something moving in the meadow. She stops chewing willow buds, raises her head slowly, and turns her long ears listening carefully. She stands motionless, transfixed on locating this new sound. She listens for her own kind. But there is no crunching of willow buds, no heavy movement of large hooves moving through snow. She barely hears the faint sound of something soft coming toward her and her calf. Her adrenalin surges as she realizes the meadow is filling with mortal danger. Her calf is resting beside her. It senses its mother's fear and stands up quickly.

The female wolf spots the two moose fifty meters away. She stops and sits down but keeps her eyes fixed on the prey. Her pack continues moving past her then they leave the moose trail forming a wide arc in front of the moose. The pack is getting excited knowing a hunt is imminent. The pups sit down in the snow and look back to their mother for the cue to attack. But she is patiently waiting for the prey to make the first move.

The cow's heart is pounding and the adrenalin is pumping, filling her muscles. She swings her giant body away from the intruders and is running now, her calf right on her heels. They are running for their lives. The female wolf lunges ahead into the soft snow. The other wolves casually watch as she passes by, then they all join in, bounding through the snow after the moose. The pack suddenly stops at the meadow edge, converging on the trail of the escaping moose. The female wolf is in the front and does not see her pack quit running. They stand and watch as she disappears into the forest.

The cow lets the calf overtake her and run ahead as they enter an open forest of spruce and aspen. The snow here is soft and shallow and their long legs move effortlessly. The calf has never run in front of its mother. It is confused and unsure of where to go. It slows until the cow is nearly over top of it. The cow senses a rapid movement closing on her flank.

The female wolf is moving quickly through the snow and gaining on the moose ahead. She has done this chase many times, and knows the cow will try to block an attack on the calf – her main target. As the wolf nears the moose, the cow spins and swings to face the attacker. The wolf dodges around a spruce tree to avoid the cow's thrashing hooves. The wolf lunges for the calf but the cow's deadly feet are there, narrowly missing the wolf's side. The wolf twists sharply and spins to safety – just in the nick of time. She tries a second time for the calf. Swinging to the left of the cow, the wolf breaks for some aspen trees then makes a hard 90^0 turn to intercept the calf. But somehow the cow is there again to block the wolf. This time the angry cow drops

her head and charges, but the wolf escapes by rolling to the right. The cow runs back behind her calf.

In a few seconds, the wolf is lunging again a meter behind the cow's broad flank. It leaps high, lands on the cow's back, and bites hard into the shoulder. But the cow bucks violently and swings her long neck back sending the wolf flying into the air. The wolf lands in a heap, but quickly scrambles to its feet and runs once more for the calf. The cow intercepts her attack, and once more the wolf jumps for the cow's back, her long canines unable to penetrate the thick hair and hide. The cow sends her sprawling into the snow again.

The wolf is beginning to tire. She has been running full speed for four kilometers - twisting, spinning, and dodging the cow. But the calf is also tiring. It has fallen twenty meters behind its mother as they run along a forested ridge. Here the calf makes a near-fatal mistake. It does not see its mother leave the ridge and head down into the heavy timber on the right. The calf continues running on then it stops when it can no longer smell its mother. It runs down the left side of the ridge and away from the cow. The calf begins to panic, running aimlessly through the heavy spruce forest looking for its mother. The wolf is walking now and has not yet given up. She climbs the ridge and follows the cow's trail down into the thick timber. The cow has heard its calf calling in the distance and moves quickly toward the sound. They reunite a kilometer away along a small creek.

The wolf finally collapses into the snow. She hears her pack howling somewhere far behind her. It is almost dark when she stands again and heads back on her trail. The other wolves have turned around and are moving up a mountain slope ten kilometers away. She travels most of the night following their trail. In the early morning she finds them resting among the boulders on a windswept mountain ridge.

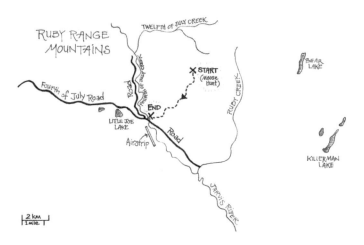

n the Yukon there is a local bumper sticker that reads, 'Eat moose, 12,000 wolves can't be wrong'. Although there may only be 5,000 wolves in the Yukon, the message is essentially correct. Moose are the bread and the butter of Yukon wolves, the fuel that fires wolf population size. Yukon wolf packs have carved up the landscape into more or less equal size ranges based on the distribution of moose. They defend this moose supply from other wolves, and they will fight to the death for the right to hunt in these territories. Why have wolves evolved such a dependence on moose that they have organized their lifestyle around this prey animal? Why are moose more important to wolves compared to caribou and Dall's sheep? The answer is simple: moose are the perfect prey. They are big-bodied prey, but wolves can easily kill young and old moose. A killed moose provides many wolf meals so the effort to hunt them is worthwhile. Moose live in small home ranges and wolves can easily find them. Wolves have figured out how many moose they need to survive and reproduce. Their territories are set by moose abundance, and the average size is about 1,000 kilometers square. If there happens to be plenty of moose in a pack's territory, pup survival is high and pack size is usually high, often ten wolves or more. If moose are scarce, few pups survive and the pack size drops to five or less wolves.

How long has this wolf dependence on moose existed, and is it the same in all regions of the Yukon? In previous chapters we found that moose became abundant in the Holocene about 8,000 years ago as forests and shrubs vegetated the mountain landscape. As the climate warmed up moose numbers increased as more and more wildfires burned, producing a mosaic of shrubs and forests that moose love.

Today, moose are found everywhere in the Yukon, but numbers are highest in the south where the density is between 15 and 25 moose for every 100 square kilometers. In the north the density is between 10 and 15 moose for the same size area.

How long have moose been abundant, and is moose history different by region? The recent history of Yukon moose can be gleaned by combining the stories of Yukon native peoples with written records of early explorers in the 1800s. It seems that moose were common in the central Yukon for a long time because native people had several different ways to hunt moose including snaring them in brush fences, or using bow and arrow to kill them at close range. In 1883, Frederick Schwatka met a group of native people near the confluence of the Pelly River. They were moose hunters, and showed Schwatka a special heavy spear they used for killing moose in the water. Other reports indicate moose were common in the central Yukon in the early 1900s. In his book *The Klondike Stampede* Tappan Adney wrote: "During the winter of 1897-98 probably 150 (moose) were killed around Dawson by Indians and white men." Charles Sheldon, another explorer, also reported moose were abundant in the central Yukon in the early 1900s. So, what does this all mean for the Yukon wolf? The Yukon timber wolf is one of the largest races in the world. I think they are large because they evolved hunting large-bodied moose and they have been preying on them for a long time, perhaps thousands of years.

Native people say moose only colonized the southern Yukon between 1875 and 1900. Before that time native people hunted caribou and mountain sheep, and rarely saw moose. Native people across the southern Yukon had no word in their languages for moose. Careless non-native trappers have been blamed for starting wildfires during the Klondike gold rush times that changed the forested landscape in favor of moose habitat – but it is more likely there were larger natural processes at work. About 1,000 years ago a large volcano erupted in the White River area depositing a broad, thick layer of ash, dust and boulders across the mountains of the southern Yukon. There is new genetic evidence that the ash layer wiped out woodland caribou in the southern Yukon and moose must also have disappeared. There has been a general warming trend in northwestern North America after the Little Ice Age ended in the early 1900s. It seems the conditions were just right for moose to invade the southern Yukon.

Early explorers in the area do not even mention moose in their journals, including E.J. Glave who first explored the far southwest corner of the Yukon in the late 1800s, and Robert Campbell who explored the southeast Yukon in mid 1800s. In fact, moose and caribou were so scarce in the Liard River basin Campbell resorted to feeding his crews fish every winter because he was unable to kill enough big game. Fifty years after Campbell abandoned his dreams of a fur post on the Liard, Warburton Pike found so many moose in the area he proclaimed it the best trophy moose area in the world. As moose suddenly erupted in the south Yukon, woodland caribou declined sharply. Elders from the Kluane Lake area remember when caribou were "black on the ice of Kluane and Aishihik Lakes." These large groups were part of the migratory Fortymile herd that numbered more than half million animals in the early twentieth century. By the 1960s the once mighty Fortymile herd was nearly exterminated by unregulated and greedy hunters in Alaska and the Yukon. Like the adaptable native peoples of the southern Yukon, the wolf also had to shift from mainly preying on caribou to moose. It seems the wolf made this essential prey switch quickly and successfully.

We found hundreds of moose kills during our research, but we rarely ever saw wolves actually hunting or killing them. The moose hunt at the beginning of this chapter is one of a handful of hunts we witnessed by following radiocollared wolves from aircraft – despite many thousands of observations. Most times we found our wolves sleeping, resting, or walking – all rather unexciting activities for a biologist. We rarely saw them hunting, but we often found wolves on freshly killed moose on our morning flights. We soon discovered that most moose kills were made in the dark winter hours. Though wolves lack the high definition and color vision of the human eye they can see exceptionally well in the dark. In this low light they see details and movements, an advantage in the Yukon where the winter daylight is less than six hours in the south, and much less in the far north.

Moose, on the other hand, do not see as well as wolves putting them at a great disadvantage at night. I often wondered why many Yukon wolves are black or very dark. I believe it is an evolutionary adaptation that camouflages them, giving them another advantage during night hunts. Yukon wolves have evolved this nightlife strategy for killing moose, and it has been quite successful judging from their kill rates. Still, hunting moose is inherently dangerous and the wolves need to be extra cautious when approaching big moose prey.

To keep from getting killed by moose, wolves use a few different approaches. The first is to force the animal to run. A fleeing moose cannot defend its flank, shoulders, and neck from wolf attacks. If wolves can get a moose running they can mortally wound it, and it can be finished off when it weakens. An experienced and healthy moose can defend itself if it stands and fights. Its chances of survival greatly improve if it does not run. The chances of surviving an attack improve more if the moose can find cover to protect itself from many-sided attacks. Trees or high shrubs can be the difference between a moose living or dying. A tree will afford protection from flank attacks while the moose's deadly forelegs can cover frontal assaults. A wolf stands a good chance of being injured or killed if it is driven into a tree by the powerful, lightning-fast forelegs of a moose. We found the battered carcass of a juvenile wolf in the Coast Mountains that made the fatal mistake of getting too close. The moose drove the inexperienced attacker into a tree trunk, then stomped it to death.

The other successful hunting strategy is extreme patience. To bring down a large moose is worth the wait. Wolves will sometimes harass moose for hours, slowly moving it from the safety of the forest into an open area where they can circle and attack it from all directions. Sometimes a pack will wait for a few days until the right moment to attack happens. We found most winter moose kills along the shores of lakes, creeks and rivers, or in large forest openings. The story of the deadly hunt is written in the snow trails. A wolf pack approaches a moose feeding on shrubs at the edge of a frozen river. The wolves separate then move into the bushes. They harass the moose out of the shrubs moving it to the river shore then onto the hard ice. Small blood spots surrounded by many wolf prints show the first serious wounding. Further along the shore a larger bloodstain shows the moose is losing the battle. Not far way, the dead moose is lying on the ice. The tracks reveal the last hours of an unfortunate moose that left the safety of the trees – and even the smallest tree can be the difference between life and death.

The Tutchitua wolf pack lived west of Frances Lake in the Finlayson area. They were one of the most impressive moose-killing packs we studied. In March 1992, I located the eleven wolves resting on top of a forested ridge on a mountain slope. A cow moose was two meters away, its back wedged tightly into a dense group of alpine fir trees. Her dead calf lay ten meters down the slope. There were no serious wounds on the cow. She stood motionless only a few meters from five sleeping wolves. As we circled I saw another moose – this one bloody and badly wounded – standing in the open alpine its back against a lonely pine tree about two meters high. The bloody snow was trampled with wolf prints in a wide area around the tree. I was certain this moose was mortally wounded and I would find it dead the next day.

I returned on the scene early next morning. All the players had not moved. The wolves still surrounded the cow in the trees. The wounded moose was still jammed up against the lonely pine, with no apparent plans to leave. The only new characters were a dozen ravens flying around the now mostly eaten calf.

When I flew back the third day the wounded moose had left the pine tree and was feeding on nearby shrubs. The cow moose was alone on the forested ridge standing next to her now completely eaten calf. The wolves had left but they were not far away, and they had been busy. Their radio signals were coming from some thick timber on the mountainside a few kilometers away. We circled and found them scattered through the forest near a freshly killed cow and calf moose. Two weeks later I happened to be flying in the same area and was curious what happened to the other moose. The cow was dead on the forest ridge above her calf. It had died only a few meters from the spot it fended off the Tutchitua wolf pack earlier. The wounded moose in the alpine had abandoned the small pine and was nowhere in sight.

The fate of a hunted moose depends not only on the landscape and vegetation around it, but also by its age and its physical condition. We visited hundreds of wolf-killed moose, collecting information on the sex, age, and condition. Most kills were of two types: either very young or very old. In the Finlayson area calves comprised about a third of the moose killed each winter. For the remaining moose, half were under four years old, and most of the others were between eleven and seventeen years old – very old ages for moose. There were few wolf-killed moose between five and ten years old, considered prime age for moose. We found a similar pattern in the Coast Mountains where calves and yearlings made up most kills, and only a few moose were in their prime. I compared the results of Yukon studies with Alaskan wolf-moose research and found the age pattern was similar in all studies. Wolves killed a lot of calves and yearlings, few prime moose, and many old ones. It seems the healthy, prime animals can usually defend themselves against wolves.

Moose calves are most vulnerable because they are inexperienced and too small to defend themselves from wolves. A calf's fate depends entirely on the skills of its mother to fend off wolves – and perhaps a good deal of luck. Nevertheless, when a pack attacks a cow and calf, the calf is usually killed. Oddly enough the cow has a survival advantage if it has a calf in winter. Wolves will kill the easiest prey so they will usually go for the calf first. If the calf is enough to fill the wolves then the cow can live another year to breed and have a new calf the next year. Still, wolves often killed cow-calf units, and even cows with twin calves.

Wolves will rarely kill a moose and not eat it. I only saw this happen twice. In March 1986 I located the Pass Creek wolves in a willow draw high in the Coast Mountains. There were two wolves lying near a live, but mortally wounded calf moose. The cow stood over it and somehow had been able to keep the wolves from finishing it off. I returned the next day and saw the cow had not moved. Her calf was alive but barely. The wolves lay in their same snow beds a few meters away. I returned for a third day, curious about the outcome of the standoff. The cow was standing beside her dead calf, but the wolves had left without feeding. I located their radio signals on a steep mountainside a few kilometers away. They had killed a Dall's sheep ram at the bottom of a high cliff. I flew by the dead calf some days later and found it covered by a deep snowdrift. The other time wolves killed a cow moose and left without eating any of it. The pack returned a few weeks later and stripped the entire carcass. The many hundreds of other moose carcasses were completely consumed shortly after wolves killed them.

There is a popular belief that wolves kill the sick and the weak, but this is a fable. Yukon wolves actually kill mostly healthy moose. We could tell the physical condition of a killed moose by the amount of marrowfat stored in their leg bones. A starving moose will have little or no stored fat. But most wolf-killed adults had high marrowfat, meaning they were not starving when they died. On the other hand, calves killed by wolves had little if any marrowfat. Calves demand a great amount of energy reserves to continue to grow in the winter, reducing their fitness and increasing the chances of being killed by a wolf pack. It is easy to understand why moose calves are such an important part of the diet of Yukon wolves.

Yukon wolf packs come in all sizes ranging from two to as many as twenty-five wolves. But what is the optimal number of wolves in a pack for hunting moose? At first thought it seems the more wolves there are the better the chance of the pack making a kill. To answer the optimal foraging size question we followed the daily activities of many different size wolf packs and figured out their kill rates on moose. In the Coast Mountains near Whitehorse we followed daily activities of fourteen packs over three winters, most for about sixty consecutive days. In the Finlayson area, we followed forty-five packs over five winters, most for about twenty days. The results were surprising.

We found single wolves can sometimes kill a moose if the situation is just right, but such events were not common. But adding one wolf turns the advantage quickly to the wolves' favor. Wolf pairs enjoy the highest amount of available moose meat per day – and much more than wolves in large packs. As pack size increases more wolves share in the bonanza and the available moose meat per wolf declines. Now you might think that the larger wolf packs simply kill more moose to even things out, but that is not what we found. Finlayson wolf pairs killed an average of twenty-seven moose, or about thirteen moose per wolf during winter. Medium size packs of four to nine wolves killed thirty-five moose, or about six moose per wolf. Packs of ten to twenty wolves killed forty-six moose, or about four moose per wolf. The results were surprising because most pairs were only young wolves, but already successful hunters. Clearly, youth did not reduce their kill rates.

Despite their young ages, Finlayson wolf pairs were already excellent hunters and did not need older wolves to help them kill moose. This is because the two adults in any pack do most of the actual killing of prey. If a moose is caught in the open the two adults will trade off attacking from different directions, harassing, tiring, and eventually bringing it down. Additional wolves may help the hunt end more quickly, and often the rest of the pack will mob a mortally wounded moose. But adults do most of the dangerous work, wounding and bringing down moose. Their pups and yearlings learn by watching hundreds of these killing events from the sidelines, avoiding injury and death until they are ready to hunt on their own.

Our kill rate studies also showed some surprising results about how long different wolf packs stay on moose kills before moving off to hunt again. All packs handled kills in only two to four days, regardless if the pack was two or twenty wolves. Pairs usually stayed the longest, but only by a day or so. But the numbers don't make sense if you calculate what captive wolves are capable of eating each day. In Chapter Fourteen we will see how two students figured out that small packs in the Finlayson area lost much more of their meat to scavengers than larger packs did, partially explaining the similar time small and large packs spent on moose kills.

Once we had determined kill rates of different size packs, we could figure out the overall wolf predation rate on moose – or the proportion of the moose removed by wolves every year. In 1994 we knew the number of Finlayson moose, the composition of all wolf packs, and their kill rates. Using this information, we estimated wolves took ten percent of the moose population that winter – a high proportion, and probably enough to keep moose from increasing. Our research shows that to really understand the predation rate by wolves on moose, biologists need to know wolf pack sizes and their kill rates. Here is why it is important. Imagine there are ten pairs in an area for a total of twenty wolves. They will kill twenty-seven moose each for a total of 270 kills. Now, if in the same area there are ten packs with ten wolves in each – five times the number of wolves – they will kill 460 moose. Pack size is everything.

So now we know something about wolf predation rate. What does it all mean to Yukon moose? Is wolf predation important or not? Our research showed wolf predation is powerful enough to hold moose at much lower levels than they could reach if Yukon wolves suddenly disappeared. Yukon moose density is naturally low and below other parts of Canada. The subarctic environment produces lower food resources for moose accounting for some of the difference. But food is not the main reason. The Yukon is a complete wilderness. In most regions the habitats are still intact and large predators arc naturally regulated – meaning people do not affect their population sizes very much. There is precious little complete wilderness left in the world. In the Yukon the combination of wolf and grizzly bear predation holds moose numbers far below what the landscape could support.

My colleague, Doug Larsen, studied causes of mortality among moose in the southern Yukon in the 1980s. Doug followed many radiocollared calves and found grizzly bears killed most of those that died before winter. In a typical year there were about 20-30 calves for every 100 cows still alive before the snow flew. Now add in wolf predation. Wolves not only kill calves but all age moose. And unlike bears, wolves do not hibernate. They spend the long winter hunting moose, a time when food resources are low and moose physical condition declines sharply making them even more vulnerable to being killed than in summer. In most years wolves will kill as many adult moose as the number of calves that make it to their first birthday. This combination of wolf and bear predation holds moose steady at low abundance. Take away these large predators and moose could reach much higher abundance.

Alaska provides a few examples of what happens when wolves and bears are removed for a long time. The Alaskans have killed wolves and bears near Anchorage and Fairbanks for many decades. Without these keystone predators moose have increased around both cities to very high numbers, up to 100 moose for every 100 square kilometers. Density is nearly seven times greater than the Yukon average of fifteen moose for every 100 square kilometers. It should be no surprise that holding predators down for long periods will produce many moose. But what is lost is the natural predator element that completes wilderness. It is wildlife farming. Is this what we want for the Yukon?

Think of Yukon moose like a yo-yo on a string and your hand is the food supply. As you throw the yo-yo down moose could increase until the string returns back into your hand, the food ceiling. Now tie a knot representing predation somewhere low down on the string. Throw the yo-yo again and moose can climb a short distance until meeting the knot. This is the predation ceiling. In the Yukon, moose numbers range below the predator knot, never able to reach the high numbers that are limited by food supply.

Wolves regulate the abundance of moose and the opposite is also true. In Chapter Eight we saw wolf numbers depend on the number of moose in an area. Wolf numbers decline as you move north matching the northward decline in moose abundance. This strong relation with moose has evolved over thousands of generations of wolves living among this perfect prey. Moose have evolved behaviors that help them avoid being killed by wolves, and wolves have adapted ways to maximize their chances of killing moose. The relation between moose and wolves in the Yukon is long one. As moose colonized the Yukon in the early Holocene, wolves stopped following migratory caribou. Wolves soon spaced themselves over the land relative to where moose lived. Packs learned the best way to protect their supply of moose was to vigorously defend their home ranges from other wolves. If moose were plentiful, wolf pup and adult survival increased and family pack sizes grew. Moose are large prey but not so difficult for wolves to kill, especially young and old ones. Compared to smaller prey like sheep and caribou, packs benefited more from killing moose because the amount of meat was much greater so wolves could spend less time traveling and hunting. We only need to look to the Kluane area where there are few moose or caribou in the high, glaciated mountains. Here wolves specialize in killing Dall's sheep, but packs are small because hunting mountain sheep is a tough life.

11

Ovis

The black wolf is just a meter behind their flying hooves - so close he can feel the tufts of grass whistling past his face and smell their warm breath. The ground is hard and good for running, but the slope is steep and uneven. In one instant the wolf is flying over small boulders, the next he is diving through shrubs, then he is running through an alpine meadow. In the dry bunchgrass his wide paws slip slightly - no match for the hard, small hooves of the sheep now rapidly outdistancing him. In a few seconds the sheep pass into a series of rocky outcrops and stop. The yearling wolf turns up the slope reaching the top of the long ridge.

He's on a narrow sheep trail along the spine winding through small boulders and meadows of low bunch grass. The south side of the long ridge is a gentle grassy meadow that extends one hundred meters below. Below the meadow, a sea of shrub birch blankets the entire mountain slope to the bottom of the valley. The sheep are running on the steep north side, hidden among a maze of huge erratics, rocky outcrops, boulder fields, and gullies that run the length of the two-kilometer long ridge. The young wolf runs along the ridge top then drops straight down the steep slope to where he last saw the sheep. The ewes are still there, and they watch the dark shape hurtling down at them through the boulders. When the wolf disappears into a shallow gully above them they escape to a large rock outcrop a hundred meters away. The wolf follows them down through the gully

unaware of dozens of sheep nervously milling among the outcrops just above. Another wolf is joining the hunt.

A few hundred meters above, three young rams are desperately trying to escape a young gray female wolf. The boulders along the ridge trail slow her down until she reaches good ground and plunges down trying to cut the rams off. She is forty meters behind them and gaining, but the rams are nearing a series of rock outcrops separated by deep gullies. They stop at the bottom of the first one, hop onto a low ledge, and climb effortlessly to the top. But the rocks are too small and the wolf scrambles up forcing the rams to run to the next outcrop. When the rams abandon the last of the rocks, they run to the base of a steep cliff perched above a dry creek wash. The cliff is thirty meters high with a series of narrow ledges chiseled into the lower face. Below, a steep gravel slope runs into the boulder-filled wash ten meters further down.

Along the cliff base are large boulders, loose rock, and shattered scree – difficult ground even for the sure-footed sheep. The rams slow to a hurried walk hopping from boulder to boulder until they reach a ledge a few meters up the cliff. One after the other the rams leap onto the ledge and nimbly turn to face the approaching wolf. She stops a few meters away and could have one in her jaws in a second. But she hesitates. She considers the risks of making a kill here. There is a large cliff below them. And the ledge above her is too narrow to make a clean kill. If she manages to get a hold of one she will certainly fall with it. She leaves the rams and scrambles uphill weaving through the rocks. She reaches the top of the cliff above the rams and disappears into high shrubs.

The rams climb the same cliff reaching a steep gravel incline near the top. They turn and look below for the wolf. Suddenly, she appears twenty meters above them hurtling down the gravel incline in a controlled fall. She tumbles and lands a meter behind the leading ram. The wolf regains its balance and lunges for the rams as they head back down the cliff. But she is losing her footing on the steep slope again. She slides down the loose scree, tumbles through the rocks, and lands in a cloud of dust at the bottom of the wash. She is bruised but not broken, and in an instant the wolf is heading for the high ridge again. She is almost on top when she surprises four rams that are heading up the ridge. But the wolf is no match on the uphill for sheep with their powerful shoulders and forelegs. They disappear and traverse the grassy slope on the other side. They are eighty meters away when she reaches the top. She heads straight for them but cannot outflank their uphill retreat.

The rams split into two groups of two. One heads east and the other west, both running below the crest. She follows the two escaping west. She stays above them and is able to cut off their escape to the ridge top. The rams begin to slow, uncertain if they should head down into the shrubs. She senses a momentary advantage and seizes it. She plunges down the hill on a sharp angle closing to thirty meters. But the rams counter by turning uphill. Her angle of attack is too shallow and she can't block them from gaining the ridge again. In seconds the two rams are above her. The rams reach the ridge top where they meet a large group of nervous sheep milling among the rocks.

The wolf is breathing heavily. She rushes into the rocks and the sheep run in every direction. As she rounds a large boulder she surprises a young ewe. The wolf lunges at it missing the white flank by a few centimeters. The ewe turns uphill to escape. The wolf spins for a second try but the ewe is already out of reach.

To the left of the wolf a dozen sheep are heading for some high rocks. She chases after three ewes but they easily outdistance her in the boulder field. They hop expertly from boulder to boulder then leap onto a cliff and scramble for the highest ledge. The wolf gives up and rushes two other ewes. They also easily avoid her by running in circles around a rock outcrop before climbing up. She circles the rock looking up at the sheep perched five meters above, too high to reach. She heads downhill again and tries for two more but they leap up to safety before she is twenty meters away. She moves quickly through the outcrops searching for one that she can surprise.

The ewe the wolf narrowly missed is hiding in a thicket of shrubs a few meters from an outcrop. The wolf heads in her direction then stops at the rocks. She can smell the ewe but she cannot see it behind the thicket. The wind is blowing through the rocks scattering scent. The wolf turns her attention to the outcrops behind but loses the scent. She abandons the dozen sheep standing on the outcrops around her, and climbs the ridge once more.

The two rams that headed east have met four others. The group is one hundred meters away when their yellow horns appear just above the ridgeline. She freezes but they have seen her moving against the skyline. She charges. The sheep turn and run back up the ridge passing by the black male wolf sitting on a grassy ledge. The sheep run down the south slope.

The male lost interest in the chase some time ago. He watches impassively as the sheep disappear below. The female approaches her mate. Her chest is pounding and she is nearly exhausted. But she is not finished. She stands beside the male for a few seconds then heads down the north side one last time. There is a large group of sheep heading for the broad valley below. She is just sixty meters behind when the group reaches the low shrubs. In minutes they are a kilometer away moving onto a mountain slope. The female walks quickly through the shrubs watching the prey disappear. She reaches the mountain and follows the scent up.

The black wolf watches her disappear. He lies down, turning his back to the wind blowing along the ridge top. Sheep are spread through the outcrops below like white sentinels. Eventually, two ewes climb down the rocks and begin to graze the short grass at the base of a large boulder. They lift their heads often to watch for the danger to return.

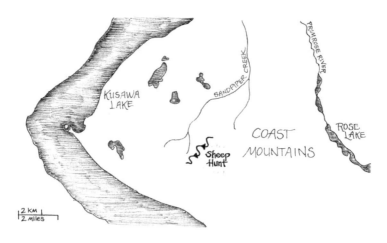

Alan Baer and Tom Hudgin watched this hunt unfold from a Super Cub. Alan wrote a detailed report that I based the story on. Alan's description of the terrain, and wolf and sheep behavior is exceptional. When I began this book I knew I would include the hunt in this chapter. In five years of following wolves in the Coast Mountains in the 1980s neither Alan nor I ever watched a successful Dall's sheep hunt. In the 1970s I watched another unsuccessful hunt, this time from the ground. As I was driving down the Dempster Highway in the north Yukon I spotted a wolf hunting two ewes near the road. The sheep climbed to the safety of a small rock outcrop four meters high. The wolf followed after them but it continually slipped on the steep rock, and could barely balance on the thin ledges. The ewes easily hopped from one ledge to another until the frustrated wolf gave up. Steep terrain saves sheep from being killed. Mountains are filled with escape terrain.

Ron Sumanik was a graduate student who did a two year study of wolf-Dall's sheep relations in the Kluane Game Sanctuary in the southwest Yukon. In the 1980s, we helped Ron collar wolves in eight packs in the St. Elias Mountains, some of the best Dall's sheep range in the world. His wolves preyed on sheep because there were precious few moose or caribou in these high, glaciated mountain ranges. Ron flew hundreds of hours relocating wolves and often saw them near sheep. He watched five sheep hunts – none were successful. Here is Ron's description of a winter hunt from his 1987 master's thesis:

"On 21 February 1985, four members of the Teepee Lake Pack were observed traversing the upper elevations of a mountain. All four animals were separate from one another. Tracks on the south slope indicated there had been much wolf activity. One wolf suddenly left the ridge and bounded down the south aspect. The running wolf generated a small avalanche of snow just ahead, similar to a boat's bow wave. Any sheep in the path of the avalanche would have been knocked down. Whether this wolf was taking advantage of the snow conditions to improve hunting success, or whether sliding snow occurred incidentally to this wolf's downhill charge is unknown. The wolf ran almost to the mountain base, passing many small, rock outcrops. Clearly this wolf was hoping to surprise and overtake a sheep among the outcrops..."

Ron watched a female wolf try killing sheep on steep cliffs on two separate hunts. Both times she walked along the cliff tops following sheep moving on ledges below. Each time she gingerly worked her way down the cliffs and came close to contacting the sheep. On the first try she lost her footing and soon retreated back to the top. On the second hunt she approached within a meter of a mature ram. The ram turned on the narrow ledge and tried to butt her with its horns. The wolf and sheep faced-off but the wolf must have reconsidered her risks. She eventually climbed back to the top of the cliff. I wonder if the wolf was trying to push the sheep to its death but soon found herself in more peril.

I think female wolves are better equipped for the complex high-speed pursuit of sheep through mountain terrain. Adult female wolves are about seven kilograms lighter than males and they can run faster. Their narrow frame can move quickly and with agility over uneven broken ground, through boulders, and down steep inclines. On a narrow ledge the smaller female can hold her balance better in tight places. Female wolves in the Coast Mountain had more broken ribs than males – the cost of pursuing the elusive Dall's sheep.

The chances of a wolf making a sheep kill are low. Sheep are highly specialized mountain herbivores. Their eyesight is exceptional, their hearing is excellent, and so is their sense of smell. They live in large groups with many watchful eyes, increasing the likelihood of detecting an approaching wolf. Dall's sheep have compact bodies, ideal for moving on steep rocks. Their hind legs are thickly muscled, and their heavy shoulder muscles enable them to quickly and easily move uphill. Their small feet are adapted for hopping onto rocky ledges that can be only a few centimeters wide. They can stand on precariously thin ledges for hours without losing their balance. They are born on cliffs, and have learned to survive by finding the balance between food, safety, and other mountain features they need to survive.

Dall's sheep use all mountain elevations during the year. They breed in early November on the lower slopes. In winter they stay on the lower slopes living near windblown canyons, cliffs, and ridges where they can find exposed grasses and sedges, and they can quickly escape from predators. In May ewes climb to the steep cliffs to have their lambs. The ewes join the other sheep and move up the mountain during summer, feeding on the newly emerging grasses and flowers. When snows arrive in September, sheep move back down the slope and begin the cycle again. A wolf needs all the advantages of surprise to kill sheep in this steep mountain world.

Wolves can kill sheep if they ambush them from above and drive them into snow, shrubs, trees, or rugged terrain where the sheep cannot outrun the wolf. Ron believes his Kluane wolves had the best chances of killing sheep when they drove sheep down into deep snow. I think he is right. This is how wolves killed the first sheep I found. In February 1983, I was flying with Danny Grangaard of the Alaska Department of Fish and Game in the mountains near Tok, Alaska. Danny is an expert snowtracker. I was on my first training flight learning how to follow wolves through sheep trails. We flew along a high mountain ridge where Danny saw wolves traveling a few days earlier. The tracks showed where the wolves chased a large group of sheep across a mountain slope. We climbed higher and circled looking to unravel the network of wolf and sheep tracks heading off in many directions. At the bottom of a long slope lay the carcass of a mature ram in a bloody snowdrift.

The tracks told the story. The wolves chased the ram off the ridge down through shallow snow. The snow got deeper and deeper, and Danny showed me the first place the ram floundered and the wolves wounded it. A hundred meters below the ram finally plunged into a deep snowdrift where the wolves killed it. In less than a day the wolves ate everything but the large horns and the backbone and moved on.

Although cliffs are usually safe places for sheep to escape to, wolves have found ways to kill them there. In the Coast Mountains we found twenty winter sheep kills made by wolves. Many kills happened on creek ice in steep canyons or at the base of a cliff. Wolves attacked the sheep and caught them before they could cross the ice and climb to safety. On ice, a sheep's hard feet have poor traction, but the wolf's broad and soft footpads hold better. We also found where wolves drove sheep from cliffs onto ice where they killed them.

Sheep hunting is dangerous for wolves and the risk of falling from cliffs is serious. Ron found a wolf badly limping near a cliff where it had been hunting sheep the day before. A young wolf in the Coast Mountain broke its leg trying to hunt sheep near a cliff. Eventually the crippled wolf could not keep up with its pack. We found its emaciated carcass a few months later, curled under a tree where it died.

In summer, sheep will forage on high grassy plateaus far from the safety of cliffs. But it is not easy for wolves to kill them even here. The sheep's great speed – especially uphill – is their main advantage over wolves. Wolves are fast, agile runners with good stamina, able to run thirty kilometers an hour for many kilometers. If they can surprise sheep far from escape terrain they stand a chance if the chase is not too steep. The wolf's long legs, lean frame, large feet, and broad tail allow it to twist and turn on a dime at high speed. But on uneven, steeply inclined ground the wolf's wide and soft footpads slip. Wolves might be able to run downhill quickly, but they do so at their own peril - often free-falling out of control. At this high speed the wolf loses agility - its key asset for taking down large herbivores. To compensate, the wolf needs to hunt often until just the right circumstance happens.

Brian Slough, a Yukon biologist I worked with in the 1980s, watched a lone wolf kill a Dall's sheep in the Ruby Range. It was August and Brian was sheep hunting and had flushed four rams earlier that day. That evening, Brian watched a black wolf approach the same rams in a high alpine valley. It chased the sheep as they retreated along the base of a mountain ridge. The rams side-hilled along the ridge and the wolf was able to close the gap singling out the oldest ram. After nearly a kilometer chase, the ram turned to face the wolf.

A Dall's sheep ram weighs about seventy-five kilograms – too small to fend off a wolf. The wolf circled the ram a few times before it grabbed it by the hind leg. The sheep tried to run but only managed to make it about thirty meters, its bloody leg torn and useless. The ram lay down while the wolf gnawed at its leg. The sheep fell into shock as the wolf began to eat it alive. The ram finally died after fifteen minutes.

Based on two wolf control experiments, wolves have little impact on whether Yukon sheep populations go up, down, or remain stable. In the 1980s, Norman Barichello, the Yukon sheep biologist at the time, surveyed sheep in the Coast Mountains where wolves were aerially controlled, and compared the response to the Aishihik area where wolves were left alone. Lamb survival was low in both areas, and both sheep populations were stable. In the 1990s we switched the experiment. This time we compared the Aishihik area where wolves were controlled to the Coast Mountains where wolves were left alone. Like Norman's study, we found no differences in lamb survival or total sheep numbers between the two areas. These experiments are the best evidence that wolves have little effect on Dall's sheep populations. Wolves simply do not kill enough sheep to make a difference to sheep population trends.

But what of the other side of the relation – do sheep affect wolf populations? To answer this we need to look at Ron Sumanik's Kluane wolf research again. Ron followed the daily movements of wolf packs to estimate the sheep kill rate. Most packs lived in the high alpine plateaus at the foot of the huge mountain peaks and glaciers where Dall's sheep was the only significant prey.

Ron found Kluane wolves had a difficult time killing enough sheep to sustain their numbers from year to year. Because sheep are small, when packs killed a sheep they did not consume much meat. The territories of sheep-hunting packs were large; pack size was small, and wolves regularly abandoned and re-colonized territories. On the other hand, packs further from the big mountains killed a mix of sheep, moose, and caribou; and did better on all accounts. Ron concluded that Kluane wolves needed more of a meat supply than Dall's sheep to survive, reproduce, and raise their families. Sheep-dependent wolves are on the precarious edge of a predation lifestyle. Sheep are too well adapted to living in the rugged mountain terrain for wolves to easily kill them. For a family of wolves to get enough food, they must kill sheep often – probably every day or so. That means they must always be on the hunt – always moving through the risky mountain terrain trying to surprise and kill sheep before they can escape to safe ground. Ron's wolf-sheep research showed wolves often try but rarely prosper against such hunting odds.

I was thankful Ron let me help him out in the field. I got to follow wolves in a prey system that had never been researched before. The north Kluane Game Sanctuary is one of the most beautiful and rugged mountain ranges in North America. Despite strong winds and harsh winter conditions, Ron pulled off a fine graduate thesis by exceptional endurance and resolve. He wrote this in his thesis, "To those who ask, 'what good is a wolf?' – I only wish ten million of you could have sat in the Super Cub with me and shared what I have seen."

Dall's sheep found a way to avoid predators by evolving a mountain lifestyle, taking advantage of rugged terrain to escape. Wolves hunt sheep but cannot rely on these small, exceptionally agile herbivores as primary prey. The wolf is well adapted for chasing down large mammals in open pursuit, but once a Dall's sheep finds steep terrain to escape to, the wolf has little chance of catching it. As a result, wolves have little affect on Dall's sheep population trends. For wolves to enjoy reasonable survival and raise their families they must have moose and caribou prey in their home ranges to supply them with an adequate supply of year-round food. There is another Yukon large mammal that has evolved a very different, migratory lifestyle that has also made it difficult for wolves to have much affect on its population.

12

The Wanderers

Spring River, Yukon North Slope – 16 June 1987

She feels them coming long before they arrive. Startled by the rumbling sound she wakes and nudges her sleeping pups off her milky belly. Deep in the den the ground begins to quake. The shaking becomes stronger until the earth around her is constantly moving. She quietly slides past her sleeping pups and crawls out of the narrow den entrance. The Arctic sun is high in the sky. The bright light momentarily blinds her as she emerges from the darkness. Her den is perched on a ledge of a steep bluff high above a fast running river. She slowly moves uphill careful to stay hidden. When she reaches the top she meets a sea of caribou. There are a thousand tightly packed animals swarming to the bluff. The nearest ones are milling a few meters from the edge, slowly being crushed forward by the mass of animals behind.

The wolf stands motionless fixed on the vanguard of cows and newborn calves. There are many she could kill but there is little room at the edge of the bluff to safely attack. The closest are only meters away. They see her and roll their eyes back in fear, shifting, jostling and pushing to escape. But they are blocked by the tide of caribou pouring in behind. There is nowhere to retreat. They shuffle along the brow of the precipice jostling to avoid the wolf and from tumbling down the steep bluff. The wolf watches as the tightly packed caribou slowly shift direction sideways. Soon the herd turns and is moving away. A handful of curious calves approach her, their noses high trying to fix on her strange scent. Suddenly there is chaos.

A wolf is racing along a tundra ridge a kilometer away breaking for the rear of the herd. In swings downhill and easily snatches a small cow by the throat. They roll over the tundra instantly breaking the cow's neck. Another wolf comes from the other direction. The caribou in the middle of the herd are confused and begin to collide together as they twist and turn to escape from the unseen danger. But they are too packed together to move. The wolf plunges headlong into the herd wrestling another cow to the ground. The wolf locks its powerful jaw into the trachea and slowly suffocates the caribou. Her calf runs away a few meters then stops. It walks calmly back to watch its mother die.

There are hundreds of caribou splintering off, and many head for the den again. The female wolf sprints forward and cuts them off, singling out a calf that is slower than the rest. She grabs it in her jaws snapping its tiny backbone. The great herd soon disintegrates as caribou find places to escape in every direction. But there are more wolves arriving. Two grays run down the escarpment and bring down a cow and her calf.

Three more wolves are chasing a large group escaping into the mountain headwaters. Another wolf appears along the bluff and intercepts a group of cows and calves climbing from out of a shallow ravine. The caribou turn just in time to see the dark shape hurtling toward them. But the wolf is running too fast. It lunges for the back of a cow. Its long canines miss and slide off the smooth hide. The wolf rolls down the ravine as the group escape across the tundra. It gives chase and closes to within ten meters of a calf desperately trying to stay with the others. The calf is strong and holds a narrow lead for more than a kilometer. As the group approaches the top of a hill they almost collide with a much larger group of caribou standing on the other side. As the wolf reaches the hill it abandons the calf and turns for the new targets heading for a broad stand of low birch shrubs. The cows fly through the meter high shrubs followed by their agile calves. The wolf cannot keep up in the bushes. After a few hundred meters it stops to watch the caribou vanish over a long ridge.

The mother wolf is standing over the dead calf and watches as the great herd of caribou disintegrates in all directions. The other wolves have ended their hunts. The caribou settle down and begin to feed again, eventually moving to the river below. Holding the limp calf in her mouth she walks back to the bluff. She settles down in a sandy hollow and begins to feed. She eats the best parts of the calf in a few minutes before slipping back into the darkness of the den. By evening the rest of the pack return to the den. The great herd of caribou has come together again as they move toward the Tulagaq River on the far horizon.

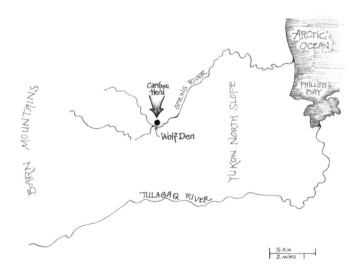

n July 1977 I spent a night with caribou biologist Don Russell camped near the Firth River near the Yukon Arctic coast. We had spent the better part of the day searching in a helicopter for a large caribou aggregation – some 10,000 animals - that had cut a broad trail across the wet coastal tundra. Unable to find the animals we decided to camp and let the helicopter pilot return to Old Crow a few hundred kilometers south. At about 2:00 a.m. I awoke to a loud clicking of hooves as thousands of caribou moved inland from the coast. Their path was right through the tent camp. The ground was enshrouded in a thick fog and the caribou began to appear in front of me like dark apparitions. I watched in silent awe as hundreds of caribou passed a few meters by my tent then disappeared behind me. It was one of the most remarkable wildlife events I ever experienced. Ten years later I began a study of the equally remarkable predator of the Porcupine caribou herd.

Arctic wolves that live in the open tundra range of the Porcupine caribou herd are vagabonds. They are unlike wolves anywhere else in the Yukon. They have no fixed home ranges and do not defend a space or territory against other wolves. Instead they follow migrating barren-ground caribou wherever that may lead. In the spring of 1987 my team darted thirty-one wolves in a dozen wolf packs to begin a wolf study in the north Yukon. By 1992 we had collared fifty-one wolves in twenty wolf packs that covered almost 50,000 square kilometers, nearly ten percent of the Yukon. Many wolves followed caribou to distant winter range then returned to the north Yukon to summer. Finding these collared wolves with aircraft was a challenge in this enormous landscape. Many collars were silent for a year or more before we found their radio signals again, often hundreds of kilometers away from where we captured them. For these wolves, home was wherever the caribou roamed.

During our wolf study, the Porcupine herd was about 160,000 caribou, but declining each year due to a pattern of low calf survival. With this huge supply of constantly moving prey there is little reason for wolves to aggressively compete for food. Territorial defense breaks down because it has no survival advantage. I was told about these wandering wolves before I began to study them. In 1986 I visited Robert Arey, an elder living in Aklavik, Northwest Territories. I wanted to know what the Tetlit Gwitch'in and Inuvialuit people understood about Porcupine caribou wolves. Over a glass of steaming tea and fresh bannock, he told me I would find many wolves following caribou in winter. He said these tundra wolves were different than the wolves on the Mackenzie Delta. They were special because they only came with caribou. They would remain in the nearby mountains so long as the caribou wintered there, then they left with the herd in the spring. Robert was right on all accounts and I was not surprised by his knowledge of wolf biology. Aklavik hunters kill wolves when the caribou come near the community, and they have done this for many decades. Arctic wolf pelts are sought after for winter park trim. A prime wolf in winter pelage can fetch more than five hundred dollars.

Migratory wolf packs converge into the wintering areas near Aklavik. In March 1992 I counted thirty-five wolves in four wolf packs hunting caribou in a small mountain creek about fifteen kilometers from the community. The valley was filled with thousands of caribou. As the caribou moved, the wolves followed like a persistent shadow. Pilot Hans Lammers followed the Porcupine caribou herd during the 1970s. He recalled seeing seventy wolves following caribou north across the Old

Crow Flats. I first thought such sightings were huge exaggerations but I now believe these are temporary collections of many traveling packs that can happen when the wandering lifestyle breaks down wolf territorial behavior.

The northern tree line divides wolf behavior in the Yukon. Migratory tundra wolves travel the treeless mountain ranges of the Northern Richardson, British and Barn Mountains. They range over more than 7,000 square kilometers following caribou everywhere they go during the year. Taiga wolves live just to the south in the lightly forested Porcupine River watershed. These wolf packs are territorial. They remain in the same general area year-round and defend their home ranges from incursions by other wolves. They range over 1,200 square kilometers similar to Yukon wolves elsewhere. Taiga wolves stay in their forested territories because there are just enough moose to hunt. But if the Porcupine herd enters their home ranges, they quickly switch to hunting the moving caribou. If the herd stays the winter, the wolves switch to hunting the great supply of caribou prey.

A wandering life sounds like an easy way for a wolf, but it is lifestyle full of risks. The Trail River wolf pack in this chapter's narrative is a good case in point. In 1987 the pack denned on the Spring River on the Yukon North Slope. That summer the Spring River happened to be at the epicenter of the Porcupine herd's calving range. A year later most calves were born far to the west in Alaska. In 1988 the Trail River pack denned 100 kilometers south of the Spring River on the Old Crow Flats. In this rich wetland complex they raised a half dozen pups on moose calves, muskrats and waterfowl – with no caribou around the whole summer.

But what made the Trail River pack decide to move their den to completely different prey ecosystem so far away? Did the pregnant alpha female anticipate few caribou would calve in the Spring River area in 1988? It need not have been premonition. She was following caribou all winter, and probably found herself on the Flats just in time for denning. That year the Porcupine herd was delayed by deep snow and many of the calves were born throughout the mountains just to the north of the Old Crow Flats. It was perfect timing for den relocation. The Flats is also a good place to intercept caribou in the fall – the time when the rapidly growing pups require plenty of food. The alpha female was in the right place at the right time in both years. She successfully raised her pups and her pack was large each year.

Making the right choice about where to den is the most critical reproductive decision Porcupine caribou wolves will make. The wrong choice means no caribou, spelling certain death for the unlucky pups. The Yukon North Slope serves up little else besides caribou. When caribou are absent the pups will starve, or the adults will kill and eat them then leave the den. That is the annual gamble migratory wolves take and it is a roll of the dice. During my study more than half the wolf breeding attempts failed, showing the high risk of relying on migratory caribou that might – or might not – show up at the den.

Life would be much simpler for wolves if caribou calved in the same place every year. But they don't. The Porcupine herd travels hundreds of kilometers from different winter ranges to calve in one of the most inhospitable places on the continent along the Alaska-Yukon North Slope. But spring weather determines exactly where they calve as we saw in 1988 – and the location is always unpredictable. By traveling long distances and changing where they calve each year, caribou have found a way to avoid most of the predators. Tom Bergerud, a noted caribou biologist, calls this behavior 'spacing away'. Tom argues that the migratory behavior of large caribou herds in Arctic Canada is a way to reduce predation by wolves and bears. His idea holds true when we look at the survival rates of calves. When Porcupine cows cannot reach the North Slope due to deep snow they will calve through the mountains to the south where there are many predators. In these years, many calves disappear shortly after birth compared to years the herd makes it to the remote North Slope where they leave most mammalian predators far behind.

Having all their calves at the same time is another way Porcupine caribou evolved to avoid predators. Cows give birth in the first week of June effectively swamping wolves with thousands of easy-to-kill calves. A wolf that makes its way to the calving grounds in June will wake up one morning to this sea of newborn calves. For a few days vulnerable calves are superabundant, far too many for wolves – and grizzly bears and golden eagles – to kill. This synchronous calving allows most newborns to develop quickly so they can escape predators. But in the first few days the killing is easy.

In early June 1979, I sat on a small mountaintop near the Malcolm River with a spotting scope, surrounded by thousands of calving caribou. I watched as a lone wolf appeared in the valley moving down the river. It began to course through the open tundra obviously hunting. It found a cow with a just-born calf. The wolf walked quickly toward the caribou. The wobbly calf ran a few meters behind its mother before it collapsed into the tussocks. The wolf went over to the calf and killed it quickly. Sometime later a large grizzly bear appeared below me. It began foraging on flower petals but I could see it was interested in something other than vegetables. As it fed it moved close to a group of nursing cows. Suddenly the bear charged the group pouncing on a day-old calf before it could stagger forward. A predator that makes it to the calving grounds enjoys a bounty of vulnerable calves, but this does not last long. Calves develop rapidly and are soon able to avoid wolves and bears. They can stand and nurse within an hour of birth and within twenty-four hours they can easily follow their mothers - and even run short distances. Within a week they run nearly as fast as their mother. Month-old calves are already fast and agile runners and can match a wolf or grizzly bear in a footrace across the tundra. In July 1977, I watched three wolves trailing a herd of about 10,000 caribou for hours along the Yukon Arctic coast. The wolves made a series of half-hearted runs at the herd but they could not kill one. Each time the tightly packed herd ran away from the wolves. The calves easily kept up with their mothers avoiding the approaching wolves.

In April 1991, Alan and I began a study to figure out how many Porcupine caribou wolves killed during the year. Flying by airplane from Aklavik, we followed the daily movements of seven radiocollared packs for three weeks. Based on twenty-three killed caribou we calculated that each wolf killed a caribou about every twelve days during winter. It turns out that this kill rate was similar to wolf research to the west in Alaska, and east in the Northwest Territories. Once we had the kill rate, I asked Don Russell, caribou biologist with the Canadian Wildlife Service, to help us with the next step. Don knew more about the seasonal distribution of the herd than anybody. For each season he estimated the size of area the herd lived in, then we estimated the number of wolves that migrated there. We calculated wolves killed 7,600 adult caribou each year. About 80 percent were killed in the fall and winter when the herd's range size was largest exposing animals to many wolves. We figured wolves killed about a third of the adults each year, and were not the most important force limiting the size of the herd.

Since 1992 the Porcupine herd has declined and is probably below 100,000 animals today. Let's assume wolves have not noticed the herd has declined and are still killing caribou at about the same rate. The predation rate could be about eight percent of the 100,000 animals. And wolves could be an increasingly important force if the Porcupine herd continues to decline even further.

I was invited by the Porcupine Caribou Management Board in 2009 to present what I knew about migratory wolves and how I thought predation might be affecting the herd. The Board was being pressured to consider wolf control to increase the herd. When asked if I would recommend broad scale wolf control I said no. I told the Board that the herd's range is enormous and is unpredictable from year to year. The herd can winter in the Yukon, Alaska or the Northwest Territories – and where they go is often a surprise to the biologists. If the Board recommended wolf control on a winter range, there is no telling if caribou will be back the next year. I advised them that the right thing to do is to leave the system alone and let it run its natural course. Porcupine wolves have lived with the herd for thousands of years and they have not caused caribou to go extinct. But there is something we can do to help the herd.

In 2010, a harvest plan for the herd was written. Non-native hunters have been under bull-only restrictions for some years. The new plan recommends voluntary restrictions on all hunting by native people throughout the herd's range. If the herd falls below 80,000 animals, much tougher native harvest rules will be applied. As I am writing this, the herd is being counted for the first time in more than a decade. The tally is still not in. There is a chance the herd may be close to the magic 80,000. If it is, the Porcupine caribou herd will be at a crossroads in contemporary management. The ethical challenge will be whether or not First Nations governments will impose legal hunting restrictions on their citizens without calling for wolf control at the same time. Killing wolves throughout the 250,000 square kilometers range of the Porcupine herd is a daunting logistical, ethical and political challenge. The scale is massive, and would involve many hundreds of wolves across three political boundaries. And, more to the biological point – such actions will have little benefit to this wandering caribou herd.

Migratory barren-ground caribou are a part of the suite of large mammal prey that Yukon wolves have evolved to hunt. Like sheep, migratory caribou have found a way to avoid wolves, limiting the effect of predation on the herd's growth. There is a good chance wolves are becoming more and more important as the herd size declines, but there is little that can be done about it except to carefully manage hunting.

Big game animals are not the only prey wolves require to survive. In summer Yukon wolves broaden their prey base to include many animals that live in a rich environment close to dens, and in winter some Yukon wolves can even find a bounty of food under ice.

13

Water

The big male wolf leaps effortlessly over the small creek and begins working his way downstream, its head low over the slow moving water. The creek winds through a large marshland lined with high willow and alders. The wolf flushes a brilliant yellow warbler, interrupting its early evening song. As the wolf moves it is intently watching the water. Twice it springs from the shore jamming its front paws into the creek and powerful jaws into empty water. The creek is moving quickly forming small eddies. The wolf stops and waits, its body poised to strike. It leaps into the shallow pool with a great splash and locks its teeth into cool and slippery flesh. It bites down until the grayling is still then walks slowly downstream a few hundred meters with it. It leaves the creek at a heavily worn trail that takes him to his den.

The den entrance is on a south facing bank overlooking the creek. The wolf steps by the skull of a Dall's sheep ram, the horns dried and decaying in the sun. The wolf walks to the entrance and stands silently with the fish in its mouth. The male wolf finds a sandy spot and lies down dropping the fish onto the ground. In a few minutes the female slips out of the den entrance, stands and stretches. She moves toward her mate, lowering her nose toward the scent of food. The male growls and the female replies in kind. She gingerly pushed her nose on the fish turning it over. She picks it up and moves a few meters away where she lays down and eats the fish in a few quick bites. She gets up and walks near the male, but he has nothing else to offer. Returning to her spot, she falls asleep in the warm sunshine.

She is wakened an hour later by a deep howl coming from the other side of the creek. The male is preparing to leave for a hunt and he begins his ritual walkabout around the den. He moves through the trails, disappearing among the willows scattered through the wetland complex. He stops and howls every few minutes, then moves to a new location. Eventually he is gone from view, working his way through the network of ponds and streams until he reaches a road. He crosses it and lets out a final howl, then strikes off for the mountain ahead. He will be hunting through the summer night.

COAST MOUNTAINS

watched this event from a forested gully on a high hill overlooking the Alligator Lake wetlands. The Alligator pack was a favorite of mine. It was one of the first packs I collared in my career. The alpha male was a beautiful cream-colored wolf, and he was the only wolf I ever saw fishing. At 13 years old, he was the oldest wolf I ever studied. I collared him about twenty kilometers north of the den a few weeks before I witnessed him fishing. When I collared him, he was scavenging from the carcass of a pregnant cow moose that was just killed by a grizzly bear. The bear slit open the uterus and ate the near-term calf, leaving a tidy pile of tiny bones beside the cow. When I chased the wolf from the carcass I had no idea it was so old. He was smart, exceptionally evasive and quick. And he nearly killed me. I continually shifted in and out of the back seat of the helicopter as I failed to get a bead on the wolf with the dart gun. In my excitement I accidentally brushed the lap belt with my forearm. I leaned out the door to aim again but found myself no longer belted in. I was balanced precariously with one foot on the exterior step and the other off the floor, with nothing but fast moving ground five meters below me. If the pilot shifted his flight path at that moment I know I would have been tossed from the helicopter thundering thirty kilometers an hour over rocky terrain. Luckily, the pilot didn't move the machine and I somehow fell back into the helicopter and eventually captured the Alligator male.

Although wolves can live as long as dogs, their wild lifestyle shortens life expectancy considerably. An 'old' adult wolf is five or six years old. They rarely live beyond their prime of life because of their hard predatory lifestyle. The Alligator male somehow beat the ecological odds by a long shot. Unfortunately, less than ten days after I watched him fishing, his luck finally ran out. Someone shot him along the Alligator Lake road, a few kilometers from the den.

Wolves breed in late February in the Yukon, and give birth about sixty days later in early May. Through the winter months the pack behaves as a cohesive family unit, free to range through their territories in search of big game animals. When spring arrives the wolf pack social dynamics suddenly change. The breeding female is heavy with pups, and can no longer travel freely. She must find a safe place to give birth to pups and raise them until they can move. The Alligator Lake pack denned in a typical habitat Yukon wolves seek out when they are ready to pup. They find wetlands.

When the pups are first born their mother cannot leave the den for a few weeks while she gives life-giving milk to her litter. She needs access to water close by to stay lactating, so you will find most dens near water. Her success raising the pups depends on her physical condition, which ultimately depends on how much food she gets from the male. In the northern boreal forest, wetlands typically produce the greatest diversity of animals, in turn providing much of the summer diet of the adult wolves. In and around wetlands is a bounty of vulnerable animals to exploit including: moose, beaver, muskrat, ground squirrels, ducks and geese, voles, mice, grayling and pike, whitefish, and salmon. About the time the pups are born, most mammals are giving birth and the ducks, songbirds and grouse are all hatching their chicks – all easy prey for wolves. The male wolf can guard the den from bears while hunting close. That way he can supply the female with regular meals while she is nursing her just-born pups. The yearlings will visit the den regularly, but they often take long hunting trips away. This is the first time they will hunt on their own without parental coaching. Biologist once thought the yearlings attended the den to help feed the new litter of pups. But the real reason they hang about is to intercept an easy meal bound for the pups.

By the end of the short Yukon summer, the pups have grown quickly and the wolves have depleted the local supply of beaver, muskrat, and moose calves in the surrounding wetlands. This is when the female moves the pups to a rendezvous area – usually another den or to an open hillside or meadow – where there is a new supply of local prey and the adults can see danger approaching. The pups stay near the rendezvous site until early October when they are fully mobile. The pups are ready to join their family in their long winter search for big game.

The most important wetlands I have seen for wolves are the Old Crow Flats of the north Yukon. The Old Crow Flats – possibly the most productive Arctic wetland in the world – provides a predictable food supply for these migratory wolves. This area contains thousands of shallow Arctic lakes that over the short spring and summer months teem with life. In spring, thousands of moose migrate to the region from their winter range in the surrounding mountains. By mid-June the lakes are dotted with bulls, cows and newborn calves. The area also supports an enormous number of muskrat, the economic livelihood of the Vuntut Gwitchin people of Old Crow for many decades. The wetlands are filled with ducks, geese and swans that come from all over North America to breed.

Between 1987 and 1990 we found seven packs denning in this huge wetland complex. We collected scats from the dens and found wolves preyed heavily on the moose calves, but muskrat and waterfowl were just as important in the wolves' diets. In August 2006, The Vuntut Gwitchin people and the Yukon government signed an agreement to protect the Old Crow Flats forever. Besides the obvious benefits to moose, muskrat and waterfowl, the conservation agreement also protects the most important denning habitat for north Yukon wolves.

Wetlands also figure large in the denning ecology of wolves in all parts of the Yukon. The Coast Mountains, southwest of Whitehorse, are a fine example. Looking down onto these rugged glaciated mountains from the air you wonder what could live below. But in most of the valleys we can find ponds, creeks, and swamps scattered along the drainages. Between 1983 and 1988, I located twelve wolf dens in these mountains. Ten were in wetland complexes. I examined over 600 wolf scats and found three important prey types: moose calves, muskrat and beaver. These are all easy prey for wolves in the summer.

Yukon wolves are also drawn to fish-rich waters for food. Pike and grayling spawn in shallow creeks in spring and wolves exploit these brief spawning runs. We found the bony skeletons of pike and other fish scattered around many dens and in scat. Wolves also feed on spawning salmon, and will even rely on salmon during the dead of winter. One wolf pack I studied stayed for weeks near a small section of the Klukshu River near Haines Junction. The river there is narrow and is bordered by high spruce trees, which made it difficult to see what the wolves were doing. The radio signals hardly moved from day to day and I was certain they must have killed at least a few moose to hang around the area for so long. After the wolves finally left the Klukshu River, I walked to the river and searched for moose kills. After an hour I realized there were no dead moose at all. Scattered everywhere along the river were dozens of decomposed salmon carcasses the wolves had dug from the ice and ate. The Klukshu River is less than twenty kilometers long, but it must provide thousands of kilograms of rich salmon for wolves to feed on during winter. Who knows how many moose are not hunted in the valley because of this bounty of dead fish available every winter.

There is also a large run of chum salmon that feeds wolves in winter along the Kluane River in the southwest Yukon. Grizzly bears and wolves feed on the salmon, but by November the river channels freeze over and the bears head to their winter dens. We studied various radiocollared wolf packs along the river in the 1990s. The salmon carcasses provided substantial food for wolves, coyotes, and foxes through the winter months.

And there is Hopkins Lake. This small lake is about forty kilometers up the Aishihik Road in the southwest Yukon. The lake is highly productive supporting many lingcod, suckers, pike and whitefish. The flow in and out of the lake is restricted, reducing the oxygen turnover. By late winter the fish have used up nearly all the oxygen under the ice. The lake slowly becomes a tomb. The fish have figured out a way to get life-giving oxygen to their gills. They swim in circles at a shallow part of the lake where they slowly erode the ice with their fins, exposing air holes where they can gulp in oxygen-enriched water. The fish jam into the air holes and become food waiting to happen.

On a wolf tracking survey I saw two wolves on the far shore of Hopkins Lake running on the ice through a maze of strange, dark objects with dozens of ravens flying above them. As we neared the wolves a macabre scene appeared ahead of the helicopter. There were carcasses of lingcod and suckers scattered everywhere on the ice – some weighing five kilograms. We collared the wolves then landed back on the lake to figure out what had happened. The wolves must have had the easiest fishing imaginable. The open shallow pools were still teeming with a knot of big fish that were oxygen-stressed, weak and easy to catch. With my bare hands I easily flipped a three-kilogram lingcod out onto the ice. Wolverine, fox, and coyote tracks were everywhere, showing other animals besides the Hopkins Lake wolf pair had discovered the good fishing hole. These isolated fish resources could have a substantial benefit to local big game. When wolves are digging for dead salmon on the Klukshu River or pulling freshwater fish from Hopkins Lake during the winter, they are not hunting moose or caribou.

Water is essential for Yukon wolves to survive. Breeding wolves need to produce milk for their pups, and as the pups grow they need to drink often. Wetlands are the most important wolf denning habitat. Much of the summer diet of the wolf pack comes from birds and mammals that live in the wetlands. Water also provides substantial fish food for some Yukon wolves in the fall and winter. But for most wolves, the winter is a time for killing big game in the snow. And an important avian scavenger has learned how to benefit from wolves and influence their kill rate.

14

Stealer

Finlayson Lake – 5 March 1990

The three ravens are gliding low over the lakeshore when they spot the carcass on the ice below. The animal is on its side, its legs splayed and head twisted awkwardly downward. The black birds twist and turn as they circle over the small bay. The three begin to call loudly over the dead caribou but they are tentative about this food. After some minutes one glides low over the carcass looking for signs of life. More ravens begin to appear attracted by the circling trio and their raucous sounds. Soon, dozens of birds are calling and circling the lakeshore. They begin to settle among the spruce trees. The bay is filled with their sharp staccato calls. But no birds will land near the food. There are no signs of the animals that kill, no howling, no blood spots on the snow. There is no trail of the big machine that leads to dead things. The birds are cautious of this strange offering that gives no clues of the owner.

Finally a raven leaves its perch, folds its wings and lands a few meters from the carcass. It faces the dead animal and calls loudly. It hops closer but is ready to fly at the slightest movement. Soon there are many more birds encircling the carcass, but none are brave enough to feed. Suddenly the air fills with the sound of a fast approaching plane. The birds leave the ice and scramble from the trees, twisting and turning through the air. The noisy plane roars above the carcass, flies out on the lake then circles back over the bay. Birds are diving into the trees weaving between the trees to escape. The plane circles a few times then disappears across lake.

Within minutes, silence returns. The ravens slowly return to their perches. A few of the braver birds land near the food. One boldly hops forward and drives its long beak into the gut tearing off a piece of flesh. As the raven flies off with its prize a handful of birds mob it as it tries to escape through the trees. A black wave of birds leaves the trees and descends onto the carcass. In minutes the caribou is covered as ravens quickly peck and pull at body parts. The first birds climb under the ribs tearing at the rich kidneys along the lower torso. Others disappear into the gut and peck through the diaphragm exposing the heart and lungs. The tenderloin along the inside of the back is shredded and removed. More and more birds arrive and peel the meat from the ribs driving their knife-like beaks in the smooth flesh. With full crops they fly off into the nearby forest and disgorge their prizes. Some hide their meat high in the crotch of spruces branches. Others slip under shrubs and push the meat down into the snow, or drop it under fallen trees. They all return quickly to the carcass. A dozen birds are tugging at the head and somehow pull the small antlers over exposing the soft neck flesh under the jaw. Within minutes the eyeballs and tongue are gone and the head is stripped of skin and muscle.

By midday the carcass has shrunk to almost nothing. The leg muscles have disappeared and the ribs are cleaned of flesh. The ravens return again and again to the shrinking caribou. They tear off strips of flesh and fly back into the trees. By late afternoon there are hundreds of secret raven caches scattered throughout the spruce forest.

Then the noisy plane returns. Like a black cloud the ravens lift off the carcass filling the sky. The plane circles once, then it disappears. The birds descend to the shattered carcass. The feeding is more difficult now. The remaining meat on the lower leg is tough and sinewy. As the daylight ends the birds begin to leave quietly in small groups. The ravens fly to the common roost they share every night in a thicket of spruce tress on a nearby mountain slope. By early evening there are a hundred birds perched among the branches. As the sun sinks they become quiet. Back at the lake there is a soft light moving along the shore. Two humans emerge from the forest and head out onto the ice. They walk to the remains of the carcass and stand over it, talking quietly.

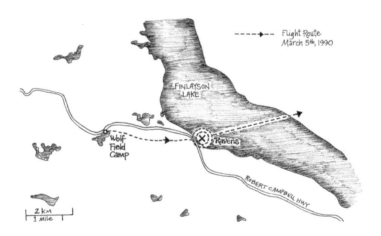

Yukon wolves will handle a whole moose in two or three days regardless of the size of the pack. So why do small packs leave so quickly? Surely it is impossible for two wolves to eat an entire moose in two or three days. Do small packs abandon kills early, leaving a lot of uneaten meat behind? Or are scavengers stealing more from small packs than from large packs? The caribou carcass in this chapter narrative was the beginning of the first field study to determine how much food scavengers steal from wolf kills.

On the morning of 5 March 1990, we slung the skinned caribou under our helicopter and dropped it along the edge of Finlayson Lake. I wanted to see how quickly ravens found it and how long it would take them to clean it up. I expected a week. I was out by six days. Less than an hour after I left the carcass I flew back over it in a plane. I counted forty ravens circling the small bay. When I retuned that afternoon the birds were still there but the caribou had mostly disappeared. I was surprised there was so little left, so I searched for tracks of wolves or coyotes thinking they must have been involved in the destruction of the carcass. But there were only raven prints on the snowy lake. Excited to see how much the ravens consumed, Alan and I drove to the lake and walked to the carcass. Everything that was edible was eaten: the heart, lungs, kidneys, and liver. The neck, legs, ribs, and back were completely stripped of flesh. Remarkably the ravens even managed to turn the head over to get at the soft flesh under the jaw. I estimated the carcass weighed about seventy kilograms when we dropped it that morning. The ravens had consumed forty to fifty kilograms leaving only the bones, hooves and skull. They ate it all in less than five hours. As we stood over the remains that evening, I knew I needed to find a student to do raven-wolf research.

Christoph Promberger was a graduate student at the University of Munich in Germany. He wanted to do a wolf research project in the Yukon and when he arrived in November 1990, we talked about possible projects. He initially wanted to look at scent-marking behavior in wolves, but I convinced him that raven research would be more interesting. I think he was at first disappointed, but he soon became immersed in his subject.

When Christoph began his research into raven scavenging you could tell when he was near by the scent of decomposing meat that followed him everywhere. My new raven researcher spent most of his waking hours in a tent frame stoking a small woodstove thawing large quarters of moose, caribou and deer that hung from the roof. Each morning he woke before dawn to set out baits before ravens began their daily search for food. Under the cover of darkness he hauled warm pieces of caribou and moose onto the lakes near camp. Then he waited for the ravens to come. At the beginning of his study, they came by but would not touch his offerings. They circled and called but they left without feeding. Ravens will quickly feed on the remains of hunter-killed carcasses in most circumstances. Something was wrong with Christoph's presentations.

After a week of failed attempts he came to me and asked what a wolf kill looks like. I explained that it looked as if a bomb went off in it. The hide is shredded and there is moose hair everywhere, the bones are broken and spread around, and the snow is bloodstained. "I think I will make wolf kills", he said. And he did. He spread moose hair and threw bones around, tossed blood or red paint in the snow, and he let his dog, Yukai, run around the lake leaving wolf-like prints everywhere. He mimicked wolf snow trails and fashioned wolf-feeding areas in the trees nearby. Then he waited. The ravens came and they began feeding in minutes.

During February and March 1991, Christoph set out seven baits and weighed them twice each day until most of the meat was consumed. He recorded the number of ravens he saw and noted tracks of any other scavengers. Christoph's research showed the word 'ravenous' was entirely appropriate for the big black birds. They quickly stripped the baits, only slowing down when the carcasses froze hard. They were far and away the most important scavengers of wolf kills. But how much food could they steal from wolves, and did wolf pack size make any difference to the amount ravens got?

The next winter Petra Kaczensky added three more baits to the sample, and she began thinking about how real wolves might interact with ravens at their kills. In 2005 Petra, Christoph and I published a paper entitled *Effect of raven scavenging on the kill rate of wolf packs*. Ravens removed an average fourteen kilograms per day from the ten baits. After estimating what captive wolves consume daily, we found this amount was too little to explain the short time real wolf packs in the Finlayson area fed on kills before moving on. To match the short time it took for all pack sizes to handle a moose we concluded ravens must steal more from small packs. I visited many moose kills over the years and rarely found wasted carcasses. To try to estimate leftovers, we weighed the remains of seven Finlayson moose kills the same day the packs moved on. All were completely consumed including two that were killed by two wolves. Ravens must have taken most of the meat because two wolves can't handle food that quickly.

Let's consider two wolves that just killed a 400-kilogram moose. There is about 260 kilograms of edible meat on the carcass. The rest is stomach contents, bone, hide and hair. Let's say each wolf can liberally consume ten kilograms of meat each day. In four days the pair can eat at most eighty kilograms of a moose carcass. That leaves 180 kilograms unaccounted for. Now, either the pairs leave most of the kill uneaten, or something else is getting the lion's share. To match the handling times of real packs, we calculated ravens must steal forty-three kilograms per day from wolf pairs, twenty-one kilograms from packs of six, but get almost nothing from packs of ten or more wolves. Our paper estimated ravens steal seventy-five percent of the moose killed by small packs, and they got less and less as wolf pack size increases. Large packs leave little for ravens because many wolves feed on the carcass, consuming it quickly.

Ravens form large flocks in winter enabling them to exploit these huge sources of winter food. I have seen as many as one hundred birds at a caribou kill, and there are often dozens of birds attending kills. How do these large flocks develop and why?

The big black birds all look the same so it seems impossible to know the age, social status, and their sex in the wild. Berndt Heinrich watched ravens in Maine and wrote *Ravens in Winter* in 1989. Heinrich was interested in the bird's social behavior. He noticed that certain birds form large flocks and called loudly whenever they discovered large carcasses, while other birds were silent. He found it was immature birds that form large flocks, calling loudly to attract more young birds to the food. The silent birds are the adults. But why would young birds want to have more friends at the dinner table? Surely, the more birds there are the less each one eats. Heinrich found young birds form large aggregations to displace adults that are defending the food sources from other birds. The secretive adult pairs remain silent around carcasses because they want it for themselves, and not draw attention to the bonanza. The mobbing behavior of immature birds evolved to allow them to successfully compete with the territorial adults for food in winter. Mobbing has had a great effect on kill rate of small wolf packs.

If you spend time at a wolf kill you will soon see ravens on the carcass, sometimes within minutes. Ravens will begin working on the head of a carcass as wolves feed a few meters away at the other end. Wolves are continually chasing birds away, but it is seems a futile comedy. As quickly as a wolf chases one raven off, another bird will appear on the other end and snatch some meat before the wolf can turn around. Just watch a pair of ravens steal food from a dog and you have the same game ravens play with wild wolves.

As much as wolves dislike ravens they also do not easily tolerate their own kind, even family members. The carcass is the centerpiece of intense aggression in the pack. To avoid the inevitable violence, wolves avoid each other at all cost and have developed a working feeding ritual. Adults feed first followed by pups, then young juveniles wolves eat last. The wolves spend as little time as possible eating at the carcass. Instead wolves slice off large pieces of meat and move to private areas away from the carcass where they can eat in relative peace. This behavior makes the carcass open for raven business – especially for small packs that spend the least amount of time at the carcass. As wolves become full they spend less time on the kill, leaving the prospects for the wily ravens. Ravens are highly intelligent and have learned all about meal planning. Ravens steal food from wolf kills for as long as they can. They hoard and hide pieces of meat wherever they can for another day. If the wolf pack is large, the ravens get little chance to feed because the wolves are on the kill much of the time, sharing the food. For small packs most of the kill goes into the stomach and crop of young ravens.

The raven is well adapted for raiding wolf carcasses. It can quickly fly over large areas in search of kills and once it finds one, its powerful beak can easily shear off chunks of meat. I witnessed the striking power of a raven beak in 1977 while studying raven behavior in the winter near Whitehorse. Dave Mossop, a Yukon ornithologist, and I caught several ravens in a large baited trap for banding. Dave caught the last bird, and wrapped it loosely under his arm. As he bent down to climb through the door of the trap the raven cocked back its head and drove its beak into Dave's glasses, shattering the lens. Had Dave not been wearing glasses he would have lost his eye.

For ravens, living with wolves is a successful survival tactic. In the Yukon wilderness there is little for ravens to eat beside wolf kills in winter, and getting to the dinner table quickly is to the advantage of the raven. During our wolf studies we often saw ravens flying above traveling wolf packs many kilometers from any kill. Knowing where the pack is helps the ravens receive as much food as possible because the birds can get food immediately.

Wolves and ravens co-evolved together since well back into the Pleistocene. Over the millennia wolves killed countless big animals providing ravens countless scavenging prospects. The idea that both animals somehow can communicate their mutual interests is not so far-fetched considering they both have elaborate vocal language. We simply cannot understand their wilderness conversations. The co-evolution of Yukon wolves and ravens has had obvious benefits to the ravens. Recognizing wolf howls and vocalizations around kills has assisted ravens to quickly find kills and compete for the spoils. But have wolves learned to recognize subtle behavior or vocal messages from the birds to help locate prey to kill? The idea of ravens communicating with wolves makes sense if you consider the long, intimate relation the two species have shared. There are some interesting stories that make me think ravens could direct wolves and help them find prey for mutual benefits.

A trapper in northern British Columbia watched ravens appear to point out the location of woodland caribou to a wolf pack traveling in winter. He saw a group of caribou cross a narrow lake and enter into a thick forest. Shortly after, a pack of wolves followed the caribou trail onto the ice. Then a large flock of ravens appeared and flew over the lake to where the caribou disappeared. They began to dive and call excitedly over the trees. The wolves walked across the lake and entered the forest under the circling ravens. In minutes the caribou bolted out of the forest and ran down the lake followed by the wolves. In *Ravens in Winter*, Heinrich tells a story of a raven that circled over a hunter calling excitedly. The hunter followed the calling bird to an unseen moose in the forest. I think it is not far-fetched to believe that ravens actively co-operate with wolves because they are highly intelligent, and they will directly benefit from kills that are made. But it is also clear that when a kill is made the wolves have no interest in sharing the spoils, and they will just as soon kill a raven as look at it.

I witnessed a strange case of ravens aggressively attacking wolves. In the spring of 1998, Denny Denison and I found a wolf pack feeding on a fresh moose kill on the Dezadeash River just inside Kluane National Park boundary. I returned the next morning in a helicopter with the wardens to radiocollar the wolves. Denny flew back to the area in his plane first, and said he would call on the radio to tell us the darting situation. The wolves had left the kill and were running a few kilometers away along a river. Then, in an excited voice, Denny said a mob of ravens was diving-bombing the wolves. We flew to where Denny was circling and came in behind the running wolves. As we approached I could see many ravens attacking the wolves, sometimes hitting a wolf on the back or head with their heavy beaks. The ravens were completely oblivious to our helicopter, and we had to be careful not to collide with flying birds as we prepared to immobilize a wolf for collaring. We darted one and in a few minutes the wolf slowed and began to stagger. All the while ravens were diving by our main rotor trying to get at the wolf. We settled down beside the wolf, but the ravens immediately landed and began pecking viciously at its head. The pilot lifted the machine back over the wolf driving the ravens off, but they did not go far above us. Denny was ahead following a second wolf and called to tell us it was in a good spot for darting. I told him to get back to us, and circle over the wolf before we dared leave it. It looked to me like the ravens were out to kill the wolf. Denny arrived shortly, and we headed downriver for a second wolf. As we were about to dart it, Denny's excited voice came over the radio again saying, "I have to land right now.

There's ravens all over this wolf and I can't keep them off with the plane."

We darted the second wolf, and this time loaded it into the helicopter for safety. We flew back to find Denny under the wing of his plane kneeling over the sleeping wolf. Like the scene from Alfred Hitchcock's film *The Birds*, the relentless ravens circled and called above us as we fixed collars on the two wolves. We stayed with them until they recovered from the drugs. The ravens eventually disappeared without doing any further harm. The cause of this strange, aggressive behavior is hard to understand. Ravens are highly intelligent birds capable of playing with other species. Yukon wolves and ravens have interacted everyday in the wilderness for thousands of years. Perhaps the age-old competition for food at the wolf kill on the Dezadeash River shifted from a playful exchange to more serious consequences for the wolves.

The raven research we conducted in the Yukon provided new insights into the important role that scavenging plays in increasing the kill rate of small wolf packs. Our studies also showed the relation between Yukon wolves and prey is a complex one that involves understanding how ravens have learned to benefit from a long association with wolves. There is a second scavenger that wolves have shared the landscape with for just as long. It is considerably more dangerous.

15

Enemy

The Babbage River, Yukon North Slope – 23 June 1980

The female wolf first sees the three bears moving slowly through the low willows along the river below. She remembers the blonde sow and feels a familiar nervousness. She walks to the edge of the low hill for a better view. The sow and her two cubs are now out of the high shrubs and traversing up the ridge toward her, grazing on the small yellow flowers that blanket the steep slope. As they get closer the wolf whimpers quietly and paces back and forth on the skyline.

The sow reaches the top of the slope and sees the wolf on the ridge. She stops and instinctively raises her nose testing the scent. The cubs crowd close to her unsure why she has stopped. Then the cubs see the dark shape above and they scramble carelessly forward. The sow huffs loudly, and slams her legs down on the tundra. The cubs spin around and rush back to her side. She turns and takes the cubs across the ridge where she might get some wind. As the bears reach the high escarpment the wolf has moved back to the den. A light evening breeze sends the wolf scent over to them. All three bears raise their noses and sniff deeply. Wolf scent is strong.

The sow recognizes the smell of this place. She moves slowly but deliberately forward, her cubs near her side. They reach the den area and stop ten meters from the hole. The wolf turns to face the bears and barks. She stares hard at these dangerous intruders with a nervous-looking grin, her mouth gaping, her long white canines showing. The sow sniffs at the ground and turns over a small scat with her nose. She moves slowly toward a fresh caribou leg bone. The cubs stop to paw at the bone.

The wolf stays transfixed on the approaching bears that are moving less than a few meters away. The tension increases as the wolf barks sharply and growls. The sow watches and considers her attack. She could charge the wolf but knows it could kill one of her two-year-old cubs. She waits, but moves slowly forward.

Just below the ridge is another bear – unseen by the animals above. It is a male boar, darker and much bigger than the sow. The bear is lying motionless in a high thicket of shrubs. A group of twenty-five bull caribou is moving through the bushes searching for a place to cross the Babbage River. They are unaware of the ambush about to happen.

The boar hears the clicking of their large hooves as the caribou approach. He knows they are close and waits until he sees the first one. He explodes from thicket, but has miscalculated somehow. The bulls are twenty meters away when they hear the willows snapping, and the dark form comes hurtling at them. Instantly the group turns and their broad hooves are churning and chewing into the fragile tundra as they scramble up the ridge.

The bear is lightning fast and is only a few meters behind the last bull, but it cannot catch it as its scramble uphill to escape. The lighter caribou quickly outdistance the heavy bear. The herd crests the high slope and runs blindly ahead.

The sow and the wolf hear something thundering up the ridge. A mass of velvet-covered antlers appears first, then dozens of caribou are charging toward them. The front bulls see them but they cannot stop. They plunge pell-mell through the den area. The sow, her cubs, and the wolf all scramble away to avoid being trampled. Then the big boar appears, hardly noticing the bears and wolf as it charges through the den after the herd of caribou. The sow runs a few hundred meters up a steep tundra hillside with her two cubs, and watches the caribou and the boar disappear beyond a distant ridge. The female wolf circles a short distance and comes back to the den.

The sow has lost interest in raiding the den. She collects her cubs and disappears down the ridge toward the Babbage River. The wolf is standing motionless above the entrance and watches the ridge for the bears to return. Soon she lies down. She can hear the muffled whining of her pups coming from the den below.

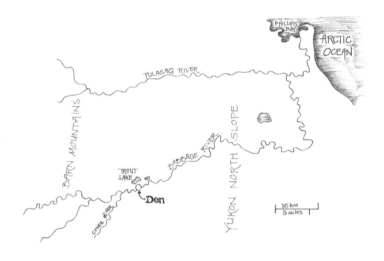

witnessed this grizzly bear-wolf encounter while I was flying a gyrfalcon survey late one evening along the Babbage River in the northern Yukon. I saw the bears from a long way off – the evening light illuminating the light blonde bears against the brilliant light-green tundra of early summer. I told the pilot to land on a small hill a kilometer away where I continued watching the scene. Through my binoculars I saw this remarkable bear-wolf encounter unfold. Incredibly, this was not the first time I saw bears trying to dig wolf pups from the same den.

I saw a similar event at the Babbage River den four years earlier. On June 10, 1976, I was onboard a Bell 47 helicopter with Dave Mossop, then the Yukon ornithologist. It was my first wolf den and Dave told me to get my camera out. As we flew up the ridge to the den, a blonde sow and her two older cubs were digging a large hole into the den entrance. Seven wolves surrounded the bears, but the wolves were rapidly losing the battle. At first I did not understand what was happening. I could not see the bears, only their heads sometimes bobbing up out of a hole. The wolves were dancing over them as they frantically jumped around the pit, lashing down at the bears. The sow stopped to swat vainly at the wolves, then continued excavating furiously into the den.

A Bell 47 is a small but noisy piston-engine helicopter. As we entered the scene we caused the bears to panic - and we probably saved the lives of the wolf pups. The bears scrambled from their diggings. The sow tried to escape, but turned and charged the wolves. They scattered a few meters back then ran for the bears heading up a low hill. Wolves jumped and bit at the fleeing bruins. A black wolf caught the shoulder of the last cub and rode it for ten meters before the young bear finally shook it off.

As the cubs escaped, the sow turned and charged the wolves again and again. But she was unable to handle them all, and her cubs soon became confused as the wolves separated them from their frantic mother. From the circling helicopter I could see that the wolves had found the upper hand. We

climbed away and watched a few more minutes then left the area as the bears continued their retreat. I returned months later to find tiny wolf scats scattered around the den area, showing there were pups hidden down below that day.

Grizzly bears and wolves are mutual enemies and the aggression has come from a long-standing competition for prey carcasses. Warren Ballard and two colleagues collected stories of 108 wolf-grizzly bear encounters witnessed by biologists. Most conflicts were over ownership of big game carcasses killed by one or the other. Bears won all the contests, much like the giant short-faced bear in Chapter One. Twenty-five other encounters were at wolf dens - including the two that I describe here. Wolves won all the den confrontations. Overall, biologists reported wolves killed grizzly bears three times, and bears killed wolves twice. There is only one published account of a bear killing wolf pups at a den. It was in the Yukon.

In 1992, Alan Baer and I published a short note in Canadian Field Naturalist titled *Brown bear preying upon gray wolf pups at a wolf den*. Alan was checking wolf den activities in the north Yukon and found the Eagle River den completely demolished as if a backhoe had worked it over. The earth had been turned over and was deeply trenched. A grizzly bear had dug into the den and killed four wolf pups. Alan found their tiny skulls neatly piled together in the trench. It was a small dessert for such a great effort by the bear. The pups would have had no chance to escape once the bear tore the roof off the den.

The greatest threat bears pose to wolves is on pups. By killing the four pups the bear wiped out the entire reproductive efforts of the Eagle River pack in 1991. But grizzly bears have a tough time reaching the pups if there are adult wolves home, as the sows at the Babbage River den found in 1976 and 1980. But adult wolves are not always around to defend the den. As the pups grow the adults will spend more and more time away hunting – sometimes disappearing for a few days. Perhaps the Eagle River adults were away hunting when the grizzly bear stumbled on the den, and it was able to leisurely dig out the pups.

Defending a wolf den from a grizzly bear is risky business. In June 1991 the breeding female of the McEvoy Lake pack in the Finlayson area was killed by a grizzly bear near her den. Alan found her and brought the carcass back to the Whitehorse lab for a necropsy. The wolf had deep wounds along her upper shoulder and skull. Alan fitted the long canines of a grizzly bear skull into the wounds and found a perfect match. The McEvoy Lake female clearly lost this fight, but the pups somehow were spared. A few weeks later we found her mate with the pups at a rendezvous site. But by early winter all the motherless pups were dead.

Despite the risks posed by bears, wolf dens are usually a safe place for wolves to raise their pups. Wolves choose dens carefully looking for physical characteristics that will protect pups from intruders. I visited more than 100 dens and I have crawled into many. Dens are usually located in soft, dry soil that wolves can easily dig deep tunnels into. The dens often face south where the summer sun can warm the soil and keep the den dry. Dens are often under tree roots, impossible for anything to dig into. Other dens are excavated in soil with large rocks making digging difficult even for bears. Many dens have smaller holes leading to it that a pup could escape through, like the pup did in Chapter Four narrative. The entrance and the tunnel are always just narrow enough for an adult wolf to slip through. I have crawled down a tunnel that was six meters long from the entrance to the chamber where the pups were raised. I had to twist my head sideways and wiggle my shoulders through a few dark places to get there. In my early years I crawled into many dens as far back as I could. I think about doing it today and I cringe with a sense of newfound claustrophobia. I am older now, and perhaps a bit wiser.

Wolves and grizzly bears co-existed in Beringia for hundreds of thousands of years learning how to defend their kills from each other, avoid conflict, and keep each other from killing their young. Wolves use their speed and agility to avoid bear attacks. Bears are simply much bigger and more dangerous contenders. Wolves must take great care in any attack on a grizzly bear. Despite sharing the Yukon landscape with bears, wolves have found good, safe places to bring up their young. Dens are located in soil that can afford protection from attacks, and the right environment to raise wolf pups.

The past eight chapters describe what I learned about Yukon wolves through extensive field research. Alan Baer and I spent thousands of hours studying how wolves fit into the large mammal complex of the Yukon. But my job did not start with research questions. When I was hired as the Yukon's wolf biologist in 1982 the territorial government wanted to kill wolves, not study them.

16

"When the facts change, I change my mind. What do you do, sir?"

John Maynard Keyes (1883-1946)

Future

Nisling River – 31 January 1997

I am in the back seat of the Jet Ranger helicopter a thousand meters over the Nisling River. In the front seat is Linaya Workman, a biologist for the Champagne and Aishihik First Nation who is working with me. We are part of a team of biologists researching how fertility control affects the behavior of wild wolves. At my feet are two unconscious wolves, both males. The biggest one is the alpha, or breeding male, and the smaller one is a

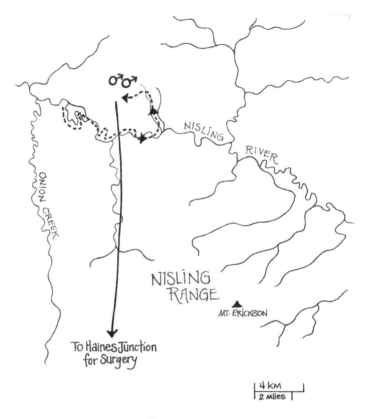

NISLING

RIVER

ONION CREEK

NISLING
RANGE

▲
MT· ERICKSON

To Haines Junction
for Surgery

| 4 KM |
| 2 miles |

It's 11:00 a.m. and -20⁰C on the airstrip. The sun has been
up for an hour. Lorne backs the pickup to the side of the
Maule LR-7 aircraft and the pilot, Denny Denison, and I take
the box down and carry it to the back door of the plane. A
film crew from Aboriginal Peoples Television Network has
arrived from Whitehorse and they start filming. They are
here to document the first study to use non-lethal methods
to control the reproduction of wild wolves. The big box
barely fits through the plane's back door, but we eventually
wrestle it inside. The alpha male is on this flight. The young
male will have to wait for the next one. Christie and Lorne

head to the helicopter base with the film crew to follow us in the Jet Ranger to the release site.

I climb in the Maule with Denny and we taxi from the apron and take off. It is a forty-five minute flight to a small lake next to the Nisling River. Denny lands the Maule on the shallow snow as the helicopter settles down a few hundred meters away. The film crew scrambles onto the lake, organizing their camera and microphones. Denny and Lorne pull the box out of the plane. They carry it fifty meters to the lakeshore and wait for the crew to film the release. When they are ready Lorne opens the box and we all wait expecting a great dash for freedom. The wolf decides to stay inside, obviously nervous. After a while, Lorne slowly lifts the back of the box and taps the side gently with his glove. The wolf suddenly is out. It runs to the edge of the lake then bounds through the deep snow into the tall trees. We all stand and watch as the camera quietly records the wolf disappearing toward the river.

I spent eighteen years studying the effects of lethal wolf control on prey populations. The science clearly shows killing wolves is biologically wrong. Killing wolves, or 'controlling' them to increase game for the benefit of people is a volatile ethical issue that deeply divides communities and Canadian society. As the Yukon wolf biologist I was on the front-line of wolf control issues for nearly two decades. I faced criticism from wolf-lovers and from wolf-haters alike – sometimes on the same day.

During my career as the Yukon's wolf biologist, the Canadian Broadcasting Company's *'Nature of Things'* produced a one-sided program that suggested Yukon wolf control was only carried out so greedy outfitters could sell more trophy hunts. The same outfitters attacked the government and biologists for closing moose and caribou hunting in their areas while wolves were being controlled. David Suzuki gave an impassioned lecture in Whitehorse calling to end wolf control, and then left without meeting with the native people who had much different opinions. During the Aishihik program, wolf interest groups from southern Canada arrived in the Yukon to protest wolf control. They burned tires on the Alaska Highway, chained themselves in the Yukon legislature, damaged our aircraft, followed me to work, and stalked my house. I had a real concern and fear for the lives of my family and crew. I lost a close friendship with a good family over wolf control that remains a raw memory years later.

At the same time there were some gratifying and poignant moments that endure and, in some ways, put the challenges I faced into perspective. I met with twenty elders of Champagne-Aishihik First Nation in 1991. They were strongly advocating for wolf control because they saw a collapse in moose and caribou in their traditional territory threatening their cultural connection to the land. At the end of the meeting an old woman came to me and said, "This is the first time someone from government has ever listened to me. Thank you."

All this for me was a great emotional conflict – trying to remain objective and scientific when many folks, understandably, have already fixed opinions about killing wolves. I hesitated when I was offered the job of Yukon wolf biologist in 1982. I was morally against killing wolves and it was clear the government was about to kill a lot of them. By accepting the job, I would be responsible for carrying out the government's directives. But virtually nothing was known about the ecology of Yukon wolves. I took the job because I saw a rare chance to understand the role of wolves in the Yukon wilderness.

In the early years I struggled with fellow biologists about the need to know something about wolves before killing them, and to understand more clearly the changing public attitude about the predator. I eventually studied a lot of Yukon wolves and came to understand many aspects of their biology including pack dynamics, reproduction, food habits, kill rates, dispersal, den selection, scavenger competition, and cause and rate of mortality. Armed with ecological information I approached wolf control as an experimental opportunity to learn as much about the wolf-prey system, and question the premise – are we doing the right thing? I worked closely with moose, caribou and sheep biologists to scientifically evaluate how different prey reacted to wolf control. As I began to better understand the wolf, I developed a clear answer to my question about the effectiveness and moral validity of lethal wolf control programs.

A friend once told me he appreciated the talks I gave in Yukon communities to explain wolf control. He said they were very objective and he couldn't tell if I was for or against it. I retired from the Yukon Fish and Wildlife Branch in 2000. I have had a decade to reflect on my experiences. A decade later I have also been able to evaluate the long-term results of wolf control programs I helped design and deliver. I can now say the benefits of broad scale killing of wolves are far from worth it – not to moose, caribou, Dall's sheep or people. It should never happen again.

Wolves have been systematically killed in the Yukon for over a century. Since the early 1900s they have been continually trapped, poisoned, and hunted. Except for some limited local benefits, early attempts at wolf control did little for Yukon moose or caribou, or for hunters for that matter. All this changed in 1982. Between 1982 and 1997 The Yukon Fish and Wildlife Branch carried out broad scale wolf control programs at great cost to taxpayers to recover moose in the Coast Mountains, and woodland caribou herds in the Finlayson and Aishihik areas. Over the fifteen years, helicopter crews shot 849 wolves in these three areas of the Yukon.

In the Coast Mountains, moose did not increase – mainly because grizzly bears, not wolves, killed most calves. In Finlayson and Aishihik, moose and caribou populations doubled or tripled as soon as wolves were reduced. After wolf control stopped, wolves recovered to normal levels in four years in all areas. If you suspend your ethics and strictly look at the numbers, you may think it was all worth it. Reducing wolves caused rapid increases in moose and woodland

Wolf study areas in the Yukon, 1982–2000

caribou. The wolves recovered quickly, and, in the end, there was plenty more game for people and for wolves to hunt. But wolf control was not worth the financial, social and ethical cost. Let's look more closely at the two successful Yukon wolf control projects and see why.

Finlayson is the longest running management program involving wolf control and prey populations in the world. Rick

Farnell, Yukon caribou biologist, started the Finlayson caribou recovery project in 1982 after traditional hunters of the herd complained they had difficulty finding the caribou. Rick counted the herd and found it was low. The Ross River native people restricted their own hunting and 450 wolves in the herd's range were killed from 1982 through 1989. By 1990, the herd had doubled in size to about 6,000 animals. Moose numbers nearly doubled at the same time increasing from 26 moose to 44 moose for every 100 square kilometers. Wolves rapidly increased after 1990, and by 1994 the population had fully recovered to 250 animals.

But the caribou herd started to slowly spiral down and by 2007 it was back to 3,000 animals. Moose also fell and by 2001 the population was only slightly higher than during wolf control years. In the end, the benefits of killing wolves to both species lasted about a decade.

The Aishihik area had similarly depressed moose and caribou populations – perhaps even lower. It had the fewest moose and caribou of any place I saw in the Yukon. The Champagne-Aishihik and Kluane First Nations, resident hunters, and big game outfitters lobbied the Yukon government to conduct aerial wolf control in 1992, citing the strong responses in Finlayson a few years earlier.

Killing 189 wolves in the Aishihik area had a profound effect on both moose and caribou. Moose increased three-fold and caribou doubled. Like Finlayson, as soon as wolves recovered in Aishihik, moose and caribou started to decline again. Both examples show that the benefits of removing wolves from the predator-prey system are brief and, upon reflection, more trouble and cost than they are worth.

But the drums of wolf control are beating again in both areas. Despite careful management of hunting in Finlayson and Aishihik, caribou and moose numbers have fallen – or they are fast on the way down. The public began complaining about low game in Aishihik ten years after the last wolf was killed. In Finlayson the complaints from hunters started after only eight years. Are we really prepared to head back into these areas and kill wolves then watch the same boom-bust happen again and again? For no matter how carefully we manage hunting, it is a biological reality that as soon as wolves recover they will pull moose and caribou down to low numbers again.

The hard news is moose and caribou are naturally at low abundance in the Yukon wilderness. This is because we are one place in the world where we still have an intact ecosystem that includes both predators and prey. Harvest, or hunting by people, simply adds to the net annual loss and drives moose and caribou even further down if it goes unchecked. This was happening in the Coast Mountains, Finlayson, and Aishihik areas before wolf control began. There were no restrictions on hunting for decades. It became harder and harder for people to find big game to hunt. Resident hunters blamed native hunters, who blamed outfitters, who blamed resident hunters. And they all inevitably pointed to wolves.

The finger pointing has been going on for the last century. And whenever game was especially low, wolf eradication campaigns appeared. This will always be the cycle unless we come to grips with the reality of natural predation. There are 5,000 wolves and as many grizzly bears living in the Yukon and the numbers have hardly changed over the last 10,000 years. Free ranging large predators make the Yukon different than most other places in the world.

Jack London and Robert Service recognized the concept of real, complete Yukon wilderness in their prose and poetry a hundred years ago and it still stands today – and I say even more so. A sense of *complete wilderness* is what the Yukon government is currently selling to tourists, and the campaign is highly successful. Today, tourism is one of the most important industries of the Yukon economy. People from all over the world come here to visit a wilderness landscape where there is little industrial change, and big predators roam freely. They may not want to meet these dangerous beasts close-up, but most tourists revel in simply knowing grizzly bears and wolves exist and they could be just around the next bend in the river. The down side is predation keeps prey populations low and there are few, if any, animals available for human hunters to take in the long run.

There are two ways to get more animals – produce more of them or reduce mortality on the ones that are already here. Improving habitat increases the physical condition of moose and caribou, which increases the number of calves that are born. In British Columbia, moose numbers have erupted after much of the old growth forests were cut down creating ideal moose habitat. These young forests produce many moose for hunters to enjoy. By comparison, Yukon forests have little commercial value and we can expect little increase in moose numbers due to habitat change, except in relation to natural wildfires.

Improving caribou habitat is a non-starter as well. More likely, warming temperatures associated with climate change will reduce the amount and quality of woodland caribou range, not improve it. The only way to achieve more moose or caribou in the Yukon is to reduce the predation rate on calves and adults. To keep prey high, predators have to be permanently controlled, an approach that I wholeheartedly reject because it would mean we would be essentially farming, not managing Yukon wildlife.

But are there other ways of controlling wolf numbers or assisting the survival of prey species? As my research took me to all corners of the Yukon, I began to understand and respect the role of wolves in regulating Yukon moose and woodland caribou herds. Wolves are not good or bad because of it. They are simply wolves doing what they have always done. A spin-off of the large amount of Yukon research has been an increase in public education about the wolf-prey system. Fortunately, a new understanding of the Yukon wolf has already started to emerge.

In 1992, an ethically diverse group of Yukoners were commissioned to produce *The Yukon Wolf Conservation and Management Plan*. The plan was a major shift from past attitudes about wolves and how to manage them. New principles included: wolves have a right to live in the Yukon, knowing wolves exist and seeing them is important to people, hunting laws should value wolves as a big game animal, and new rules should be met before wolves are controlled to increase big game. Among other things, the plan recommended researching non-lethal methods to control wolf numbers. As the Yukon biologist at the time, I saw fertility control as the only viable method to maintain low wolf numbers, but nothing was known about how it might work in wild wolf populations.

We began investigating fertility control in the Aishihik area in February 1994 by performing a vasectomy on one male wolf. The wolf was returned to its mate and they failed to breed for two years but remained together and held their territory. The vasectomy did not seem to have affected the pair's social behaviors. Encouraged by the result, the Champagne-Aishihik First Nation, a partner in the Aishihik project, approved full-scale research on wolf fertility control on December 20, 1995. In January 1996, Christie Spence, a graduate student from University of Toronto, joined us to lead fertility-control research on Aishihik wolves. This was the first research of its kind in the world.

Between January 1996 and February 1997, we helped Christie capture seventeen wolves and flew them to Haines Junction and Whitehorse where they could safely undergo surgery. Veterinarians performed vasectomies on males and tubal ligations on females. After wolves recovered we returned them to the same area they were captured. Then Christie watched how they behaved back in the wild.

Christie found the surgeries did not affect their natural behavior. She studied seven wolf pairs that included surgically treated males and females. All but one pair failed to reproduce, and all pairs stayed mated. They traveled and hunted together, defended their territory, and behaved like other wild wolves. The surgeries were safe, but the male vasectomies were easiest and least complicated to perform. Christie constructed a population model and concluded fertility control could help moose and caribou increase.

Christie and I were invited to Alaska to give advice about the value of fertility control as a way to increase big game. Buoyed by the success in Aishihik, the Alaska Board of Game endorsed more research in that state. An international planning team recommended a similar approach to recover the Fortymile caribou herd in 1997. Between the 1920s and 1973 the Fortymile herd collapsed from nearly a half million to about six thousand animals, a victim of severe weather, predation and overharvest. The recovery plan included harvest closures in the Yukon and Alaska, and Alaska biologists live-captured and moved 140 wolves off the herd's range. Fifteen wolf packs were surgically sterilized on the summer range. Calf survival immediately increased and the herd grew to 43,000 animals by 2003, the first real growth the herd had seen for many decades.

Another Yukon-Alaska herd was successfully increased without any type of wolf control. The Chisana caribou herd rapidly declined from 1,800 animals in 1987 to about 700 animals in 2003. Few calves survived each year, and the adults in the herd were rapidly aging. There was real concern the herd would disappear if the trend continued. The herd ranged through U.S. and Canadian national parks, so there was no option for using wolf control.

Yukon biologists Michelle Oakley and Rick Farnell designed an innovative way to increase calf survival that worked beautifully. Between 2003 and 2005, they captured a total of 115 pregnant cows and flew them to a ten hectare, fenced enclosure and held them there from March through June. The natural forage in the enclosure was supplemented with hand picked lichen and commercial reindeer ration. The cows gave birth inside the fence that was designed to keep wolves and bears out. Once the calves were old enough they were released and their survival was compared to wild born Chisana calves. Survival rate of enclosure calves was about 75 percent compared to just over 10 percent for their wild cousins.

The Chisana caribou recovery project shows there are ways to help threatened wildlife without resorting to wolf control. The financial costs are high and the question that remains is – how committed are we to applying these new methods?

After nearly twenty years of working with wolves, I know they will not be left alone simply because reducing their numbers will have only short-term benefits to big game. Yukoners will continue to hunt moose and caribou. Land claim agreements recognize the rights of First Nation citizens to hunt for subsistence needs. Outfitters provide a substantial income to the Yukon economy. Many Yukoners, myself included, enjoy hunting and fishing, and it is one of the reasons why we live here. We can expect that whenever game is low there will be calls to reduce wolves. There will even be some people that will want to regularly schedule periodic wolf control to keep game high.

The fundamental question we must ask is: do we want complete wilderness, or do we want to have some form of continuous or periodic wolf control in areas to augment human harvest of moose and caribou? The Yukon Fish and Wildlife Management Board is a public advisory group tasked with developing public direction about wildlife issues. The Yukon Government and the Board are currently reviewing the *Yukon Wolf Conservation and Management Plan*. I hope they reject broad scale wolf control in favor of leaving wolves alone. If they support continuing wolf control, I hope they will choose non-lethal or smaller scale methods. There are possible solutions to increasing moose and caribou, but they require a major rethinking about how we manage our landscape and the wildlife that live on it.

Moose numbers are lowest and concerns are greatest near Yukon communities where most harvest is centered. Special areas could be designed around these communities where a handful of wolf packs are trapped and the surviving wolves are held down by fertility control for long periods. This form of wolf control requires strong community participation. It could only happen by ending the archaic trapline ownership restrictions that give a few trappers the exclusive rights to trap areas around communities, or not. Trapping methods need to be researched to ensure the most humane methods are used.

For caribou herds, the alternative is more complex. Woodland caribou herds have large annual ranges. Our recovery approach in Finlayson and Aishihik was to reduce wolves throughout the entire range of the herds. But an equally strong response in the Fortymile caribou herd happened when wolves were transplanted and new pairs were surgically sterilized on the herd's summer range only. The Chisana caribou experiment was successful because Yukon biologists thought of a completely different approach for recovering a small, threatened herd – moving cows to a safe enclosure, and allow them to raise their young without predators. The Yukon has come a long way from bounties in the 1930s, poison campaigns in the 1950s, and aerial control in the 1980s-1990s. But are we headed for the future?

Rick Farnell wrote a legacy paper in 2009 reflecting on his three decades as Yukon caribou biologist. He describes seeing a 'paradigm shift' in how to recover woodland herds. I worked closely with Rick and we share many of the same conservation perspectives. The shift, he writes, started with intense aerial wolf control in Finlayson. Then it moved to wolf fertility control in Aishihik, strong regulation of harvest, public education campaigns to protect habitats, and finally captive rearing of wild caribou in Chisana. A handful of other forward-thinking biologists enabled these innovative management projects to happen for moose and caribou, including Alan Baer, Rick Ward, Gerry Kuzyk, Jean Carey, Rob Florkiewicz, Lorne LaRocque, Christie Spence, Michelle Oakley and Dorothy Cooley.

There has been a great amount of predator-prey research in the Yukon since 1982, more than anywhere else in Canada. I worked with other biologists designing research that revealed the nature of wolf-prey relations, and the short-lived benefits of wolf control to prey. We asked fundamental science questions:

What can we learn by changing the natural predator-prey system? Will moose and caribou increase when wolves as removed? How long will increases last? What generates the population growth, increased calf or adult survival, or both? Do moose, caribou, and Dall's sheep respond the same way? Have we done the right thing? Are there better ways to manage the system? Some of the answers were immediate and some took many years. While we were asking these science questions, other forces were moving public policy into the future.

Planning teams integrated our science to inform societal decisions. These included the Yukon Wolf Planning Team, the International Fortymile Planning Team, and the half dozen U.S. and Canadian partners involved in the Chisana captive rearing project. The Champagne-Aishihik, Kluane, and White River First Nations became partners to find innovative non-lethal ways to increase traditionally important wildlife populations. Environmental groups did their part to help shift public policy, but the real change came from ordinary Yukoners. The common thread in all voices was questioning wolf control as the only solution for increasing big game populations. I believe science has answered the question of the periodic, broad scale wolf control. It has limited benefit to prey populations, it does not last, and should be relegated to the past along with poison and bounties. So what is the future of the wolf then?

Despite the constant challenges the wolf has faced since the Pleistocene it has endured and succeeded in becoming the primary force shaping the Yukon wilderness today. It has survived prey extinctions since the ice age. When their main prey disappeared, wolves promptly found new mammals to hunt. Genetics shows Yukon wolves apparently disappeared at the end of the Pleistocene, but a new race immediately reoccupied the

Yukon landscape. In the last hundred years the Yukon timber wolf has recovered from trapping, hunting, bounties, poison, and aerial control campaigns. Despite this persecution the wolf has endured.

There are as many wolves ranging through the Yukon today as there were a hundred years ago, a thousand years ago, five thousand years ago. They live everywhere around us, and sometimes come into our communities and kill pets and livestock when natural prey is down. Like gray wolves around the world, Yukon wolves are shy and intelligent and are no threat to our personal safety. Few people today trap and hunt wolves, and even if there were more interest it would have little effect on wolf numbers in the long run. No, the wolf is not at risk of disappearing from the Yukon. Its future depends on how Yukoners and other people around the world view our place in this vast mountain wilderness, and how much of it we are willing to protect and share with this exceptional predator and its prey.

Suggested Reading

I have included some of the most interesting and important books, periodicals and journal articles that form the background of each chapter. Refer to authors in the bibliography for source details. For a comprehensive and up-to-date review of all aspects of wolf biology and ecology see Mech and Boitani (2003).

Chapter One – The Mammoth Steppe

Kurten and Anderson (1980) remains the best source for Pleistocene mammal descriptions. Although outdated, the book is the reference for nearly everything Pleistocene. For a comprehensive and excellent description of the ecological change at the end of the Pleistocene read Pielou (1990). Guthrie (1990) is a good reference book about the large mammal complex of the mammoth steppe. Guthrie does some fine forensic detective work figuring out which predator killed Blue Babe. For two opposing views of the nature of the giant-short faced bear, read Matheus (2001) for the ferocious, and Figueirido and others (2010) for the placid. Fox-Dobbs and others (2008) is a seminal isotope study identifying Pleistocene diet of keystone herbivores and carnivores.

Chapter Two – The End of Horses

Stay with Pielou (1980) for a fine description of the revegetation and reanimation of North America after the ice sheet melted in the Pleistocene-Holocene transition period. Guthrie's short paper in Nature (2006) is a good summary of when and why Beringia mammals went extinct – and it's only three pages long. It is rather dry, but Kennedy and others (2010) describes the phenomenal flooding of the Porcupine watershed in the north Yukon, and its eventual draining away. Leonard and others (2007)

Bibliography

Adney T. 1994. The Klondike Stampede. University of British Columbia Press, Vancouver. Originally published in 1900 by Harper and Brothers Publishers, 463 pages.

Ballard W.B., L.A. Ayers, P.R. Krausman, D.J. Reed and S.G. Fancy. 1997. Ecology of wolves in relation to migratory caribou herds in northwest Alaska. Wildlife Monographs 135, 47 pages.

Ballard W.B., L.N. Carbyn and D.W. Smith. 2003. Wolf interactions with non-prey. Pages 259-271 in Wolves: Behavior, Ecology and Conservation, edited by L.D. Mech and Luigi Boitani. University of Chicago Press. Chicago.

Barichello N., J. Carey, R. Sumanik, R.D. Hayes and A.M. Baer. 1989. The effects of wolf predation on Dall's sheep populations in the southwest Yukon. Yukon Renewable Resources Report. Government of the Yukon, Whitehorse.

Barnett R., B. Shapiro, I. Barnes, S.Y.W. Ho, J. Burger, N. Yamaguchi, T.F.G. Higham, H.T. Wheeler, W. Rosendahl, A.V. Sher, M. Sotnikova, T. Kuznetsova, G. F. Baryshnikov, L.D. Martin, R. Harington, J.A. Burns and A. Cooper. 2009. Phylogeography of lions (Panthera leo spp.) reveals three distinct taxa and a late Pleistocene reduction in genetic diversity. Molecular Ecology 18, pages 1668-1677.

Barnosky A.D., P.L. Koch, R.S. Feranec, S.L. Wing and A.B. Shabel. 2004. Assessing the causes of late Pleistocene extinctions on the continents. Science 306, pages 70-75.

Bergerud, A.T. 1989. Caribou, wolves, and man. Trends in Ecological Evolution 3, pages 68-72.

Bergerud, A.T. 1992. Rareness as an antipredator strategy to reduce predation risk for moose and caribou. Pages 1008-1021 in Wildlife 2001: Populations, edited by D.R. McCullough and R.H. Barrett. Elsevier Applied Science, New York.

Berton P. 1972. Klondike: The Last Great Gold Rush 1896-1899. Anchor Canada, 472 pages.

Clayson D. 2007. Encounter with wolves. Pages 29-30 in From first we met to the internet, edited by Yukon College. Whitehorse.

Cruikshank J. 1990. Life Lived Like a Story. University of Nebraska Press.

Dale B.W., L.G. Adams and R.T. Bowyer. 1995. Winter wolf predation rate in a multiple ungulate prey system, Gates of the Arctic National Park. Pages 223-230 in Ecology and conservation of wolves in a changing world: Proceedings of the second North American wolf symposium. Canadian Circumpolar Institute, University of Alberta, Alberta.

Fancy S.G., and K.R. Whitten. 1991. Selection of calving sites by Porcupine herd caribou. Canadian Journal of Zoology 69, pages 1736-1743.

Fancy S.G., K.R. Whitten and D.E. Russell. 1994. Demography of the Porcupine caribou herd. Canadian Journal of Zoology 72, pages 840-846.

Farnell R. 2009. Three decades of caribou recovery programs in Yukon: a paradigm shift in wildlife management. Department of Environment, Government of the Yukon, Whitehorse,18 pages.

Farnell R. and R.D. Hayes. 1992. Results of wolf removal on wolves and caribou in the Finlayson study area, 1983-1992. Department of Renewable Resources Report, Government of the Yukon, Whitehorse.

Farnell R., P. G. Hare and D. R. Drummond. 2005. An ancient wolf den and associated human activity in the southwestern Yukon Territory. Canadian Field Naturalist 19, pages 135-136.

Farnell R., P. G. Hare, E. Blake, V. Bowyer, C. Schweger, S. Greer and R. Gotthardt. 2004. Multidisciplinary investigations of alpine ice patches of southwest Yukon, Canada: paleonenvironmental and paleobiological investigations. Arctic 57, pages 247-259.

Figueirido B., J.A. Pérez-Claros, V. Terregrosa, A. Martín-Serra and P. Palmqvist. 2010. Demythologizing Artodus simus, the 'short-faced' long-legged and predaceous bear that never was. Journal of Veterinary Paleontology 30, pages 262-275.

Fox-Dobbs K., J.A. Leonard and P.L. Koch. 2008. Pleistocene megafauna from eastern Beringia: Paleoecological and paleoenvironmental interpretations of stable isotope and nitrogen isotope and radiocarbon records. Palaeogeography, Palaeoclimatology, Palaeoecology 261, pages 30-46.

Fryxell J.M., J. Greever and A.R.E. Sinclair. 1988. Why are migratory ungulates so abundant? The American Naturalist 131, pages 781-797.

Gasaway W.C., R.D. Boertje, D.V. Grangaard, D.G. Kelleyhouse, R.O. Stephenson and D.G. Larsen. 1992. The role of predation in limiting moose at low densities in Alaska and Yukon and implications for conservation. Wildlife Monographs 120, 59 pages.

Gasaway W.C., R.O. Stephenson, J.L. Davis, P.E.K. Shepherd and O.E. Burris. 1983. Interrelationships of wolves, prey and man in interior Alaska. Wildlife Monographs 84, 50 pages.

Glave E.J. 1890 and 1891. Our Alaska Expedition. Frank Leslie's Illustrated Newspaper, New York.

Griffiths B., D.C. Douglas, N.E. Welsh, D.D. Young, T.R. McCabe, D.E. Russell, R.G. White, R.D. Cameron and K. Whitten. 2002. The Porcupine caribou herd. Pages 8-37 in Arctic Refuge Coastal Plain Terrestrial Wildlife Research Summaries, edited by D.C. Douglas, P.E. Reynolds and E.B. Rhodes. U.S. Geological Survey, Biological Resources Division, Biological Science Report USGS/BRD/BSR-2002-0001.

Guthrie R. D. 1990. Frozen Fauna of the Mammoth Steppe: The Story of Blue Babe. University of Chicago Press, Chicago, 323 pages.

Guthrie, R.D. 2006. New carbon dates line climatic change with human colonization and Pleistocene extinctions. Nature 441, pages 207-209.

Gwitch'in Renewable Resource Board. 1997. Nanh' kak Geenjit Gwitch'in Ginjik: Gwich'in Words About the Land. Gwitchin Renewable Resources Board, Inuvik, 212 pages.

Hare P.G., S. Greer, R. Gotthardt, R. Farnell, V. Bowyer, C. Schweger and D. Strand. 2004. Ethnographic and archaeological investigations of alpine ice patches in southwest Yukon, Canada. Arctic 57, pages 260-272.

Harrington F.H., L.D. Mech and S.H. Fritts. 1983. Pack size and wolf pup survival: Their relationship under varying ecological conditions. Behavioral Ecology and Sociobiology 13, pages 19-26.

Hayes R.D. 1987. Wolf population research and management studies in the Yukon, population inventories 1985-87. Yukon Fish and Wildlife Branch Report, Government of the Yukon, Whitehorse.

Hayes R.D. 1995. Numerical and functional responses of wolves, and regulation of moose in the Yukon. Department of Biological Sciences thesis, Simon Fraser University, 132 pages.

Hayes R.D. and A.M. Baer. 1992. Brown bear, Ursus arctos, preying upon gray wolf, Canis lupus, pups at a wolf den. Canadian Field Naturalist 106, pages 381-382.

Hayes R.D. and A.S. Harestad. 2000a. Demography of a recovering wolf population in the Yukon. Canadian Journal of Zoology 78, pages 36-48.

Hayes R.D. and A.S. Harestad. 2000b. Wolf functional response and regulation of moose in the Yukon. Canadian Journal of Zoology 78, pages 60-66.

Hayes R.D. and D.E. Russell. 1998. Predation rate by wolves on the Porcupine caribou herd. Rangifer Special Issue No. 12, pages 51-58.

Hayes R.D. and D.H. Mossop. 1987. Interactions of wolves, Canis lupus, and brown bears, Ursus arctos, at a wolf den in the northern Yukon. Canadian Field Naturalist 101, pages 603-604.

Hayes R.D., A.M. Baer and D.G. Larsen. 1991. Population dynamics and prey relationships of an exploited and recovering wolf population in the southern Yukon. Yukon Fish and Wildlife Management Branch Final Report TR-91-1. Government of the Yukon, Whitehorse, 67 pages.

Hayes R.D., A.M. Baer and P. Clarkson (unpublished). Ecology and management of wolves in the Porcupine caribou range, Canada. For copy contact author.

Hayes R.D., A.M. Baer, U. Wotschikowsky and A.S. Harestad. 2000. Kill rate by wolves on moose in the Yukon. Canadian Journal of Zoology 78, pages 49-59.

Hayes R.D., R. Farnell, R.M.P. Ward, J. Carey, M. Dehn, G.W. Kuzyk, A.M. Baer, C.L. Gardner and M. O'Donoghue. 2003. Experimental reduction of wolves in the Yukon: ungulate responses and management implications. Wildlife Monographs 152, 35 pages.

Heard D.D. and T.M. Williams. 1992. Distribution of wolf dens on migratory caribou ranges in the Northwest Territories, Canada. Canadian Journal of Zoology 70, pages 1504-1510.

Heinrich B. 1989. Ravens in Winter. Vintage Books, New York, 379 pages.

Hopkins D.M., J.V. Matthews Jr., C.E. Schweger and S.B. Young, editors. 1982. Palaeoecology of Beringia. New York: Academic Press, 489 pages.

Kaczensky P. 2007. Wildlife value orientations of rural Mongolians. Human Dimensions of Wildlife 12, pages 319-329.

Kaczensky P., R.D. Hayes and C. Promberger. 2005. Effect of raven, Corvus corax, scavenging on the kill rates of wolf, Canis lupus, packs. Wildlife Biology 11, pages 101-108.

Kaufman D.S., T.A. Ager, N.J. Anderson, P.M. Anderson, J.T. Andrews, P.J. Barlein, L.B. Brubaker, L.L. Coats, L.C. Cwynar, M.L. Duvall, A.S Dyke, M.E. Edwards, W.R. Eisner, K. Gajewski, A Geirsdóttir, F.S. Hu, A.E. Jennings, M.R. Kaplan, M.W. Kerwin, A.V. Lozhkin, G.M. MacDonald, G.H. Miller, C.J. Mock, W.W. Oswald, B.L. Otto-Bliesner, D.F. Porchinu, K. Rühland, J.P. Smol, E.J. Steig and B.B. Wolfe. 2004. Holocene thermal maximum in the western Arctic (0-180⁰W). Quaternary Science Reviews 23, pages 529-560.

Kennedy K.E., D.G. Froese, G.D. Zazula and B. Lauriol. 2010. Last glacial maximum age for the northwest Laurentide maximum from the Eagle River spillway and delta complex, northern Yukon. Quaternary Science Reviews 29, pages 1288-1300.

Kuhn T., K.A. McFarlane, P. Groves, A.Ø Mooers and B. Shapiro. 2010. Modern and ancient DNA reveal recent partial replacement of caribou in the southwest Yukon. Molecular Ecology 19, pages 1312-1323.

Kurten B. and E. Anderson. 1980. Pleistocene Mammals of North America. Columbia University Press, New York.

Kuzyk G.W., D.E. Russell, R.S. Farnell, R.M. Gotthardt, P.G. Hare and E. Blake. 1999. In pursuit of prehistoric caribou on Thanlät, southern Yukon. Arctic 53, pages 214-219.

Larsen, D.G., D.A. Gauthier and R.L. Markel. 1989. Causes and rates of moose mortality in the southwest Yukon. Journal of Wildlife Management 5, pages 548-557.

Leonard J.A., C. Vilà, K. Fox-Dobbs, P.L. Koch, R.K. Wayne and B. Van Valkenburgh. 2007. Megafaunal extinctions and the disappearance of a specialized wolf ecomorph. Current Biology 17, pages 1146-1150.

Lescureux N. 2006. Toward the necessity of a new interactive approach integrating ethnology, ecology and ethology in the study of the relationship between Kyrgyz stockbreeders and wolves. Social Science Information 45, pages 463-478.

London J. 1990. The Call of the Wild, White Fang and Other Stories. Oxford University Press, New York, 362 pages.

Matheus P.E. 2001. Pleistocene predators and people in eastern Beringia: did short-faced bears really keep humans out of North America? Pages 79-101 in People and Wildlife in North America: Essays in Honor of R. Dale Guthrie, edited by S.G. Gerlach and M.S. Murray. British Archaeological Reports International Series 944.

McCandless, R.G. 1985. Yukon Wildlife, a Social History. University of Alberta Press, Edmonton, 200 pages.

McLellan, Catherine. 1987. Part of the Land, Part of the Water. Douglas and McIntyre Limited. Vancouver, 328 pages.

McLellan, Catherine. 2001. My Old People Say, an Ethnographic Survey of Southern Yukon Territory, Part 1. Mercury Series, Canadian Ethnology Service Paper 137. Canadian Museum of Civilization. 324 pages.

Mech L.D. and L. Boitani. 2003. Wolves: Behavior, Ecology and Conservation. University of Chicago Press, Chicago, 448 pages.

Mech, L.D and L. Packard. 1990. Possible use of wolf den over several centuries. Canadian Field-Naturalist 104, pages 484-485.

Miller F.L., A. Gunn and E. Broughton. 1988. Surplus killing as exemplified by wolf predation on newborn caribou. Canadian Journal of Zoology 63, pages 295-300.

Murie A. 1944. The Wolves of Mount McKinley. Fauna of the National Parks of the United States, Fauna Series No. 5, 239 pages.

Peterson, R.O. and P. Ciucci. 2003. The wolf as a carnivore. Pages 104-130 in Wolves: Behavior, Ecology and Conservation, edited by L.D. Mech and L. Boitani. University of Chicago Press, Chicago.

Peterson, R.O. and P. Ciucci. 2003. The wolf as a carnivore. Pages 104-130 in Wolves: Behavior, Ecology and Conservation, edited by L.D. Mech and L. Boitani. University of Chicago Press, Chicago.

Pielou E.C. 1991. After the Ice Age. University of Chicago Press, Chicago, 366 pages.

Pike W. 1967. Through the Sub-arctic Forest. Arno Press, New York. (Original publication 1896).

Russell D.E., K.R. Whitten, R. Farnell and D. van de Wetering. 1992. Movements and distribution of the Porcupine caribou herd, 1970-1990. Canadian Wildlife Service Technical Report 138, 139 pages.

Schwatka F. 1983. Along Alaska's Great River. Northwest Publishing Company, Anchorage, 95 pages.

Selous F.C. 1907. Recent Hunting Trips in North America. Scribner's, New York.

Service R. 1990. The Best of Robert Service: Illustrated Edition. Running Press Book Publishers, Philadelphia, 199 pages.

Sheldon C., 1911. The Wilderness of the Upper Yukon. T. Fisher Unwin, London.

Smith B.L. 1983. The status and management of the wolf in the Yukon Territory. Pages 48-50 in Wolves in Canada and Alaska: Their Status, Biology and Management, edited by L.N. Carbyn. Canadian Wildlife Service Report Series 45.

Smits C.M.M. 1991. Status and seasonal distribution of moose in the northern Richardson mountains. Yukon Fish and Wildlife Branch Report TR-91-2, Government of the Yukon, Whitehorse, 63 pages.

Spalding D.J. 1990. The early history of moose Alces alces: distribution and relative abundance in British Columbia. Contributions to Natural Science, Royal British Columbia Museum, Victoria, 11 pages.

Spence C.E. 1998. Fertility control and the ecological consequences of managing northern wolf populations. University of Toronto thesis, Toronto.

Spence C.E., J.E. Kenyon, D.R. Smith, R.D. Hayes and A.M. Baer. 1999. Surgical sterilization of free-ranging wolves. Canadian Veterinary Journal 40, pages 118-121.

Stephenson R.O., S.C. Gerlach, R.D. Guthrie, C.R. Harrington, R.O. Mills and G. Hare. 2001. Wood bison in late Holocene Alaska and adjacent Canada: paleontological, archaeological and historical records. Pages 125-159 in People and Wildlife in North America, Essays in Honor of R. Dale Guthrie, edited by S.G. Gerlach and M.S. Murray. British Archaeological Reports International Series 944.

Sumanik R.S. 1987. Wolf ecology in the Kluane region, Yukon Territory. Michigan Technological University thesis, Houghton, 102 pages.

Thomas D.C. 1995. A review of wolf-caribou relationships and conservation implications in Canada. Pages 261-273 in Ecology and Conservation of Wolves in a Changing World: Proceedings of the Second North American Wolf Symposium. Canadian Circumpolar Institute, University of Alberta, Edmonton.

Walker F. 1978. Jack London and the Klondike. The Huntington Library, San Marino, California, 288 pages.

Walsh N.E., B. Griffith and T.R. McCabe. 1995. Evaluating growth of the Porcupine caribou herd using a stochastic model. Journal of Wildlife Management 59, pages 162-172.

Williams T.M. 1990. Summer diet and behavior of wolves denning on barren-ground caribou range in the Northwest Territories, Canada. University of Alberta thesis, Edmonton, 75 pages.

Wilson W. 1970. Campbell of the Yukon. Macmillan Company of Canada, Toronto.

Workman W.B. 1974. Prehistory of the Aishihik-Kluane area, southwest Yukon Territory, Canada. University of Wisconsin thesis, Ann Arbor.

Wright A.A. 1976. Prelude to Bonanza. Gray's Publishing Limited. Sidney, British Columbia. 321 pages.

Yukon Wolf Management Planning Team. 1992. The Yukon wolf conservation and management plan. Yukon Renewable Resources Report, Government of the Yukon, Whitehorse, 17 pages.

Zazula G.D. G. MacKay, T.D. Andrews, B. Shapiro, B. Letts and F. Brock. 2009. A late Pleistocene steppe bison (Bison priscus) partial carcass from Tsiigehtchic, Northwest Territories, Canada. Quaternary Science Reviews 28, pages 2734-2742.

Recent History of Wolves

1903	Jack London publishes *Call of the Wild*
1904	Market hunters reduce moose and caribou herds
1920	Trappers licensed to use poison
1929	Wolf and coyote bounty
1931	Poison outlawed, but illegal activity continues
1933	Wolf bounty repealed
1930s	Highest recorded wolf harvest ever
1942	Alaska Highway construction, big game decline sharply
1946	Wolf bounty reinstated
1949	*Look* magazine criticizes Yukon game laws
	Yukon Game and Publicity Department established
1952-1956	Kjar's strychnine poison pellet campaign
1953	Wolf bounty repealed
1956-1958	Fuller's strychnine poison bait campaign
1972	Poison use restricted
1982-1985	Coast Mountains moose recovery – aerial wolf control
1983-1989	Finlayson caribou recovery – aerial wolf control
1985-1986	Kluane wolf-sheep study
1987-1992	North Yukon wolf study
1990-1995	Finlayson wolf recovery study
1991-1992	Finlayson raven study

1992	Yukon wolf conservation and management plan
1992-1998	Aishihik aerial wolf control experiment
1996-1997	Aishihik wolf fertility control study
1997-2002	Fortymile caribou recovery – wolf fertility control
2003-2006	Chisana caribou captive rearing experiment

Photo Credits

Lorne LaRoque (LL), Petra Kaczensky (PK), Ulrich Wotschikowsky (UW), Brian MacDonald (BM), all others by author.

Photo inside cover:

A seventy kilogram male wolf, Coast Mountains. The largest Yukon wolf known by author.

Collection of colour photos (read them clockwise for details):

Page 1

Wolf pack traversing Ark mountain, southern Yukon (LL).

Page 2, 3

Main prey species of Yukon wolves: Porcupine caribou, moose, snowshoe hare, Dall's sheep (PK), woodland caribou (UW).

Page 4, 5

Wolf capture: Helicopter above the Yukon North Slope. Wolf radiocollars. Extracting blood for disease study. Pat Maltais and author radiocollaring wolf. Alan Baer darting (UW). A perfect darting shot (UW). Lorne LaRoque collaring Finlayson wolf. North Slope crew collaring wolf in Northern Richardson's Mountains.

Page 6, 7

Landscape and pilots: Helicopter chasing wolf in subalpine Coast Mountains. Typical U-shaped mountain valley caused by glaciation, Frances Lake, Finlayson (UW). Pilot Denny Denison and his Maule LR-7. Helicopter capturing a wolf from Wolverine Lake pack, Finlayson. Pilot Tom Hudgin and his Super Cub PA-18.

Page 8, 9

Typical wetland used by denning wolves, Dempster Highway, northern Yukon.

Page 10, 11

Predation: Carol Domes and Gerry Kuzyk examining wolf-killed moose (BM). Radiocollared wolf that died from unknown causes, Finlayson (UW). Wolf-killed moose, Finlayson. Pilot John Witham, Petra Kaczensky and author weighing carcass of a wolf-killed caribou, Finlayson (UW). Raven researcher Christoph Promberger at wolf-killed moose, Finlayson. Wolf attacking cow and calf moose, Aishihik (see narrative Chapter Ten). Wolf moments after crawling out of moose carcass (BM).

Page 12, 13

Kluane Range, southwest Yukon.

Page 14, 15

Landscape and people: Typical subalpine habitat for woodland caribou, Ogilvie Mountains. Limestone ridge used by Porcupine caribou herd during migration, Old Crow area, north Yukon. Wolf den in natural meadow, Coast Mountains. Native youth on snowmachine, Ross River, Finlayson (UW). Ulrich Wotschikowsky and trapper Steve Peconi with wolf pelt, Finlayson Lake (UW).

Page 16

Trail of six wolves crossing lake, Coast Mountains.

Acknowledgements

Many wolves were killed to form the ecological basis of Yukon research. Killing wolves was never easy, and their lives were never taken without remorse. I also acknowledge the hundreds of radiocollared wolves that we chased down and captured for study. I sincerely hope the disruption to their lives was worth gaining a better understanding their complex world.

I thank my family for helping me produce this book. Kelly Milner, my daughter, edited the book. My other daughter, Aryn Madley, was my researcher. My brother, Barrie Hayes, drew the illustrations between practicing law. Others assisted in production. Grant Zazula, Yukon paleontologist, reviewed prehistoric chapters. Todd Fuller wrote the Foreword. Regine Zimmerman designed the book and did the layout. Stephanie Ryan drew the maps. Philip Merchant took the cover photograph. Lorne LaRocque, Petra Kaczensky and Ulrich Wotschikowsky provided color photographs and Richard Bernt formatted them. Ulrich helped with book design, editing and helped coordinate printing in Germany.

The following pilots flew thousands of hours in difficult and often dangerous mountain conditions in winter: Denny Denison, Tom Hudgin, Derek Drinnan, Cameron Drinnan, Ray Harbats, Jim Buerge, Rob Pyde, Rob Lawson, Jim Hodges, Norm Graham, Doug Makkonen, John Witham, Matt Conant, and John Fletcher. Thanks to you all for keeping all of us safe. I thank Bob Cameron for advice about Yukon aviation details in Chapter Seven.

Many people helped with field and other research including Alan Baer, Philip Merchant, Patrick Maltais, Peter Koser, Christoph Promberger, Petra Kaczensky, Jean Carey, Dave Bakica, Daryl Anderson, Ulrich Wotschikowsky, Ron Sumanik, Aryn Madley, George Balmer, Norman Barichello, Kevin Bowers, Dan Drummond, Donna Milne, Morris George, Harvey Jessup, Doug Larsen, Susan Westover, Rhonda Markel, Heather McLeod, Barney Smith, Greg Hare, Rick Ward, Ken Frankish, Hanna Hoefs, Janet McDonald, Rick Farnell, Peter Clarkson, Graham Baird, Dorothy Cooley, Ilme Liepens, Kevin Bowers, Judy Selamio, Don Russell, Doug Larsen, Lorne LaRocque, Linaya Workman, Christie Spence, Rich Weir, Mike Dehn, Kathi Egli, Gerry Kuzyk, Mark O'Donoghue, and Brian Slough.

I also thank veterinarians Jim Kenyon, Darrell Smith, and Michelle Oakley for performing wolf surgeries.

Wildlife research cost money and working on wolves requires considerable political support. I thank the following people with providing both: Hugh Monahan, Don Toews, Doug Larsen, and Brian Pelchat.

I had three mentors in my career. Bob Stephenson taught me about wolf management. William Gasaway encouraged me to go back to school to become a better biologist. Alton Harestad of Simon Fraser University helped me become one.

Most of all, thanks to Caroline.